Poppin' With W

Stunning Flying Geese Quilts with a Pop!

By
Tina Dillard

Printed in the United States of America

Editor: Yvonne Fuchs

Cover Design, Interior Design, Illustrations, and Photography: Robert and Tina Dillard

Published by Quilting Affection Designs

www.quiltingaffection.com

Dedications

I want to dedicate this book to my loving and supporting family;

Robert, Patrick, Colton, and Maria

I also want to thank my Mom and Aunt Sharon for passing their love of quilting and sewing on to me!

Thank you!

Acknowledgments

I would like to acknowledge the following individuals and companies for their help and support in the development of this book. I want to start by thanking Deb Tucker and the Studio 180 Design team for providing support for me as I wrote this book and for allowing me to use their tools. Also, I want to thank the ladies from Running with Scissors Quilters. They were the collaborators along with Studio 180 Design in the development of the Corner Pop II and III tools. If it weren't for these tools, we would not be able to develop beautiful and exciting quilts like the ones found in this book.

I also want to thank my dear friend and Longarmer Januari Rhodes, The Quilted Ginger. You recognized my potential as a designer and encouraged me to write this book. When I needed it, you were there to challenge me and pushed me to heights that I could have never achieved without your encouragement. Additionally, I want to thank you for taking the time out of your busy days to help me tweak the quilts and make them beautiful. Finally, I will never forget the Fall Market 2019 road trip and how we talked out the ideas for writing the book.

I would like to thank fellow Studio 180 Design Certified Instructor, Carolyn Ratola, Cat's Quilting for taking her time to look over and edit drafts of this book before we went into testing phase. Also I want also to thank the other Studio 180 Design Certified Instructors, who took time to test all the projects in this book.

Thank you to Ebony Love, Love Bug Studios, for the great book coaching and support I received during the Book Camp. The information was incredibly useful; it kept me on track.

Finally, I want to put in a huge thank you to my husband, Robert Dillard. He has been my most significant support system and helper to get this book together. If it weren't for his help in this book, developing the cover images and reviewing every part of the book, I would have never finished on time. I couldn't have asked for a more supportive and talented husband.

Contents

Foreward

Whoever believes that there is nothing new in the quilting world will have to rethink that message once they explore Tina's book. Her use of our tools, the Wing Clipper and Corner Pop II and III, is eye opening, not just for me, but for all of us here at Studio 180 Design! She stretches the boundaries and explores beautiful designs using some revolutionary machine piecing construction techniques. Her collection of projects is certain to delight both the modern and traditional quilt makers among us. What looks impossible, becomes simple with Tina's step by step, illustrated instructions. You will certainly be amazed at what awaits you when you venture into any of the "Poppin' With Wings" projects.

Deb Tucker
Studio 180 Design Founder and Creative Kingpin

Quilting creates a family with a common thread. It is the artistic expression of the love, hope, and joy we each look for in our daily lives. The rhythm of the designs brings us joy. The promised result of stitching various shapes of fabrics to form a new whole embodies hope. The warmth and beauty of each quilt provides a practical expression of the love we feel for others. It fulfills us.

In this book, Tina shares her quilting vision of love, hope and joy. The clear instructions, unique designs, and the promise of fabrics assembled into beautiful, artistic quilts shows that Tina's Quilting Affection Designs is well-named. We look forward, as you will, to more creative works from this quilt artist.

Ellen, Heidi, and Kathy
Running With Scissors Quilters

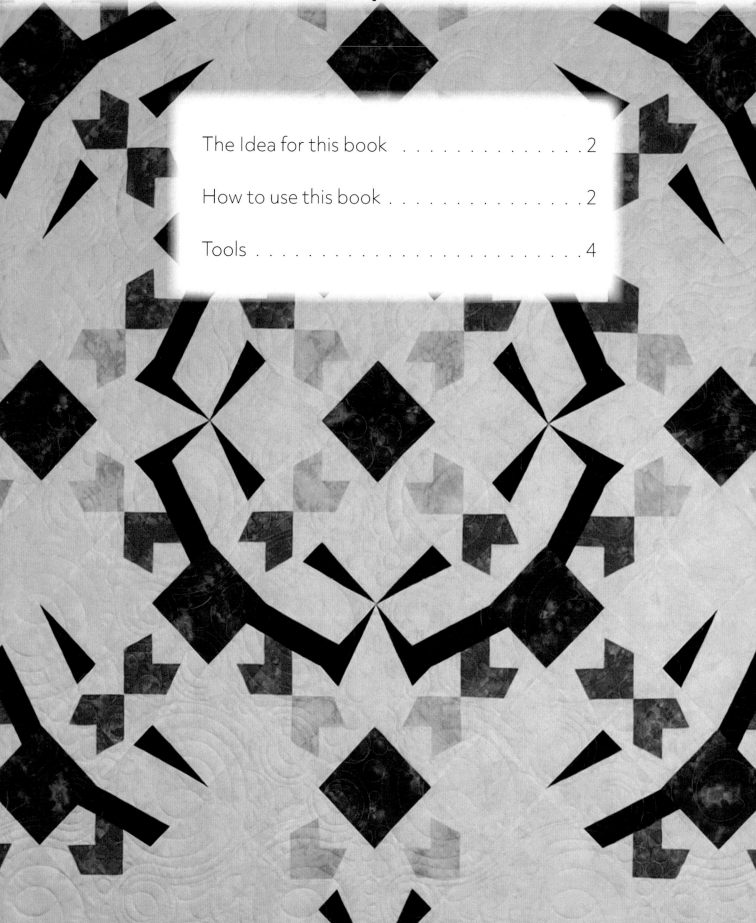

Chapter 1

The Idea for this book

The idea for this book first came up while traveling to the 2019 Fall Quilt Market with my friend and show volunteer, Januari. Initially, it was just a rough idea and a focus on some of the techniques that I use in the patterns I develop. As time went on and after a few bumps in the road, the idea was refined. I decided to focus on the concept that Januari and I started. I took the flying geese unit and gave them an extra kick by using the Studio 180 Designs Corner Pop II and Corner Pop III tools. Then using EQ8 quilt design software, several ideas sprang to life, which makes up the basis of this book.

I love the flying geese block, a common unit that is the base of many beautiful quilt designs. My goal with this book is to take the flying geese unit to the next level and show you what can be done by adding corner pops to them. The simple step of popping the corners and adding triangles creates an entirely different unit. It expands the variety of designs that can be produced. What makes this so exciting is that it is an amazingly easy process to follow. By taking the Wing Clipper®, Corner Pop® II, and Corner Pop® III from the library of tools from Studio 180 Design, a fantastic set of patterns will spring to life built around flying geese units.

After learning the Corner Pop techniques with the combination of flying geese, you have a great starting point to build upon. Using the Corner Pop® II and Corner Pop® III, new life can be brought to any basic unit. I believe this will open you up to new design possibilities and will bring new life to even old quilt patterns. That is why I am so excited to see this book come to life and share the techniques. The sky is the limit when it comes to what is now feasible.

How to use this book

All the Projects in this book are created using the Studio 180 Design Wing Clipper® I and the newest Corner Pop® II and III tools and techniques. These tools are required to make the units and can be purchased through your local quilt shop, the Studio 180 Design website (https://deb-tuckers-studio-180-design.myshopify.com/) or my website (https://quiltingaffection.com/). Each of the tools contains step by step illustrated instructions to show you the process of how to use them and includes illustrations for both left and right hand cutting. If you need additional instructions, you may want to watch the Studio 180 Design free on-line tutorials on the Wing Clipper and the Corner Pop® II and III tools.

Purpose

The purpose of this book is to use both the Wing Clipper® and either the Corner Pop® II or III tool together in a project. There are eight projects in this book divided by either the Corner Pop® II or III tools. Chapter 4 contains four projects that feature the Wing Clipper® and Corner Pop® II tools. Chapter 5 has another four projects using the Wing Clipper® and the Corner Pop® III tools.

I have also provided a General Instructions chapter, which can be found on page 2. This chapter is broken down into two sections that offer you detailed step by step instructions on how to use the tools. The first part of the chapter covers the Wing Clipper, showing you how to

How to use this book Continued...

make the various types of Flying Geese, and the Picket technique. Additional instructions follow on how to trim the units to the correct size using the Wing Clipper® I tool. The second half of the chapter walks you through the process of how to pop the corners of the units and the use of the Corner Pop® tools.

Chapter 3, Putting It Together, walks you through the process of assembling your quilt and how to put the borders on correctly.

Fabric

The fabric I used came from my local quilt shop and were from various companies and are mostly made with their basic fabric collections. Please support your local quilt  shop first when shopping for fabric and supplies. You can follow my fabric choices, or I challenge you to get creative and add your own personal touch. I provided a gray scale image of the quilt to help you understand the fabric values.

Project Page Breakdown

The Project Pages are broken down into sections to help you stay on track throughout the process of making each quilt. Each project starts with the project size, unit summaries, and the amount of yardage you will need. The yardages are based on 40" width of usable fabric (WOF), plus I have added a little Oops factor into the yardage (we all make mistakes). Then in each of the patterns, I provide color illustrations showing you the units that will be made along with step by step instructions.

Cutting Chart

The cutting chart includes easy to follow information for cutting and preparing fabric for your project. Each chart has fabric color, how many to strips to cut, and sub cutting instructions. The sub cutting also lets you know how many Types I and II Replacement Triangles you will need to cut.

Each of the projects is broke down into the following areas:

- Replacement Triangle Cutting
- Flying Geese Construction
- Popping Units
- Block Assembly
- Quilt Assembly and Borders

I break these projects out into small manageable sections so that they can be done a little at a time. This will help keep you from feeling overwhelmed while working. I want you to have fun and enjoy every step of your quilt making experience.

Tools

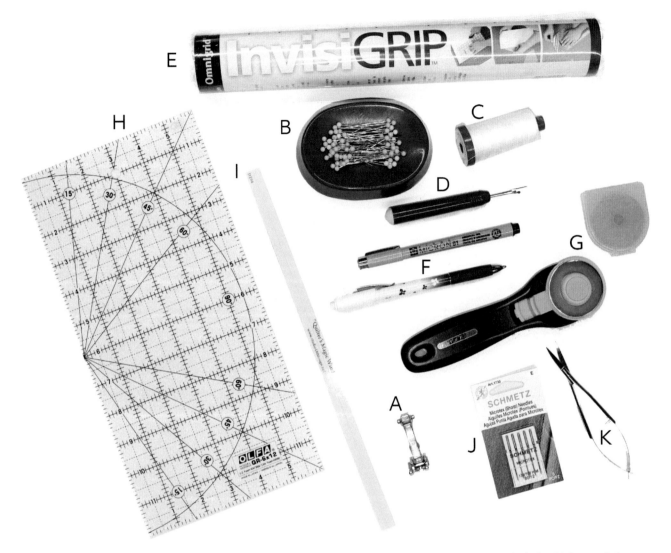

A. ¼" Foot *B-D.* Additional tools and accessories *E.* InvisiGrip *F.* Marking Tools *G.* Rotary Cutter and Blades *H.* Rotary Rulers
I. Quilter's Magic Wand *J.* Sewing Needles *K.* Snips

Along with having a sewing machine in good working order, you will need a few tools to create the projects.

Studio 180 Design tools

You will need the Wing Clipper® I, and one or both Corner Pop® II and III tools by Studio 180 Design. You can purchase them from your local quilt shop, visit the Studio 180 Design website (deb-tuckers-studio-180-design.myshopify.com/) or my website (quiltingaffection.com).

Each of the tools comes with additional instructions on how to use your tools. These instructions include charts and easy to follow steps with illustrations for both left and right-handed cutters. Please read through the instructions thoroughly, practice each of the steps to get familiar with the techniques, so you understand the design concepts.

InvisiGrip™

InvisiGrip™ is a thin clear plastic that you place on the back of your tools to help prevent them from slipping on your cutting mat while you are cutting. The plastic adheres to your tool by static cling, so there is no adhesive element used. This makes the product easy to change out when it gets dirty and needs replacing. InvisiGrip™ will also prevent nicks and scratches on your tool and will help prevent the fine lines on the back of your tools from fading away. I highly recommended to covering your tool from edge to edge. You can find InvisiGrip™ at your local quilt shop with other quilting notions, and it comes on a roll that can cover several tools.

Quilter's Magic Wand

The Quilter's Magic Wand is a wonderful tool that provides you with an exact ½" reference. This ruler has an etched line running down the middle that gives you an accurate ¼" on each side. The Quilter's Magic Wand is used when high precision is required such as marking for Flying Geese lines.

Marking Tools

When it comes to marking tools for your project, I recommend using a fine line mechanical pencil, such as Sewline Fabric Pencil or a fine pen such as the Ultra-Fine Pigma Micron 01 pen. Make sure your marking tool is easy to see and will give you a nice fine line at the same time.

Rotary Rulers

These thick acrylic rulers are made especially to be used with your Rotary Cutter and Cutting mat.

In addition to the Studio 180 Design tools, it is recommended that you have standard rotary rulers that measure 6" x 24" and 6" x 12". The 6" x 24" ruler is great for cutting strips that are the Width of Fabric (WOF) and for large blocks. The 6" x 12" is great for sub cutting all your strips into squares. I also recommend having a 12" x 12" or larger square ruler, for squaring up blocks.

Another tool I use to subcut my units is the Studio 180 Design Tucker Trimmer® I, II, and III tools.

Rotary Cutter and Mats

A good quality rotary cutter and mat are highly recommended for any quilting project you do. When I am cutting out my pieces for my project, I prefer to use a 45mm rotary cutter. The 45mm will allow you to cut up to four layers at a time. My favorite is the OLFA brand rotary cutters. Ergonomically they feel the best in my hand, plus they have a comfortable grip and a safety latch. Please remember safety when you are using any rotary cutter. I recommend to close or retract the blade every time you set your cutter down on the mat. Safety first!

Also, remember to wipe down your blade and cutter periodically to clean off any excess fabric and lint. I like to change my blades out before starting any new project. I recommend having a large supply of new blades.

Iron and Ironing Surface

Having a good clean iron and ironing surface is key to getting a crisp seam and to get blocks to lay flat. I use a lint roller periodically over my ironing surface to keep the loose threads from fusing to it. Each day before you start, check your iron before turning it on. Wipe off any excess dirt and lint. If your iron plates are dirty, refer to your iron instructions to clean the surface.

Mary Ellen's Best Press

When I'm setting my sewing seams, I use Mary Ellen's Best Press™. This product will not leave flakes on your fabric. I pour my Best Press into a mister bottle. The mister bottle will allow you to spray a fine mist of the fabric sizing evenly.

Additional tools and accessories

Beyond the specific tools above, you'll need some general quilting items such as a 100% Cotton 50 wt. Thread, needles, ¼" piecing foot, scissors/snips, pins, seams ripper, etc. Remember when buying your supplies to look for the best quality equipment you can afford. Doing this will make you happier with your final product.

Chapter 2 - Studio 180 Tools

Wing Clipper

The Wing Clipper® is a fundamental tool that is used to trim down traditional Flying Geese units. This tool will allow you to trim down 10 different size options and get your oversized units to the exact size you need with the seams going directly into the corners.

Flying Geese

There are a lot of ways to make Flying Geese units for your projects. In this book we will be concentrating on the No Waste Method for all but one of the projects. In that project, we will be using the Stitch and Flip Method, so instructions for both techniques are included.

The No Waste Method uses four small squares (wings) and one large square (body) to make four Flying Geese units. The Stitch and Flip method is great for when you need to make one unit at a time and/or you need to have two different wing colors that need to be on a specific side. As always with everything in the Studio 180 Design units are mead oversize and then precision trimmed to the desired size.

The trimming will be done using the Wing Clipper® I tool to give you precise and crisp looking units, quickly and accurately. This trimming process will be used for both of the methods.

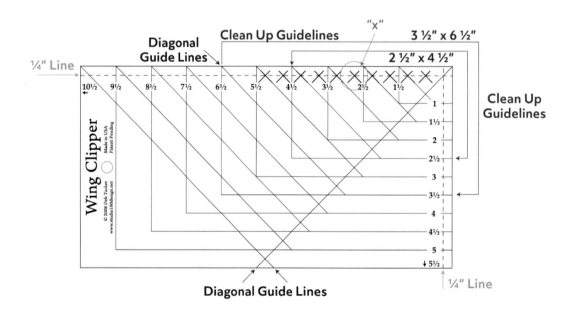

Note: *The Flying Geese sizes we will be using in this book are the following:*

Finished	Cut Size	Small Squares	Large Squares
2" x 4"	2½" x 4½"	Small Squares – 3"	Large Squares – 5½"
3" x 6"	3½" x 6½"	Small Squares – 4"	Large Squares – 7½"

No Waste Flying Geese Method

1. Gather four small squares / one large square that are required for the project you are making.

Step 1 - Gather

2. Using your Quilter's Magic Wand™ and a fine marking tool, mark two lines, each ¼" away from the center diagonal on the wrong side of the small squares.

Step 2 - Mark

3. Position two small squares diagonally on opposite corners on a large square as shown. Nudge each small square toward the center about 2 or 3 threads from the raw edge of the larger square.

Step 3 - Position

4. Stitch on the drawn lines, then cut apart between the lines of stitching on the center diagonal.

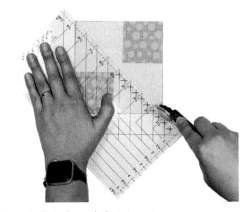

Step 4- Stitch and Cut Apart

5. Press seams in the direction indicated by arrows.

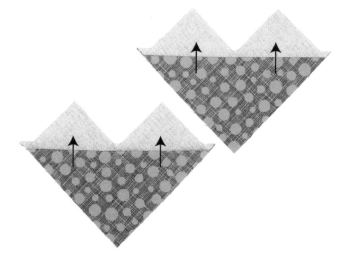

Step 5 - Press

6. Position one small square on each unit and nudge 2 or 3 threads from the raw edge of the larger triangle section.

Step 6 - Position

7. Stitch on the drawn lines, then cut apart between the lines of stitching on the center diagonal.

Step 7 - Stitch

8. Press seam toward the small triangle.

Step 8 - Press

9. Trim according to the directions on page 12.

Stitch and Flip Flying Geese

This method is used in the Petal Spinner project on page 98.

1. Gather one rectangles and two squares that are required for the project you are making.

Step 1 - Gather

2. Using your Quilter's Magic Wand tool, mark a sewing line from corner to corner diagonally on the wrong side of the squares.

Step 2 - Mark

3. With right sides facing, position a square with the rectangle, assuring the center line runs from the lower left to the upper right.

Step 3 - Position

4. Stitch on the drawn line, then trim ¼" away from the sewn line. Press seam toward the triangle.

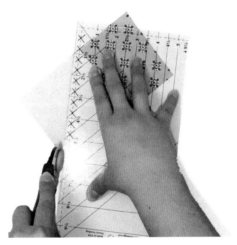

Step 4 - Stitch, Trim and Press

Stitch and Flip Flying Geese

5. Place the remaining square on the opposite side, assuring the center line runs from the upper left to the lower right.

Step 5 - Place

6. Stitch on the drawn line, then trim ¼" away from the sewn line. Press seam toward the triangle.

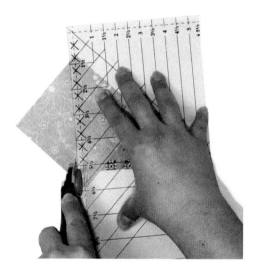

Step 6 - Stitch, Trim, Press

7. Trim according to the directions on page 12.

Trimming Process

Right-Handed

1. Position the oversize flying geese unit horizontally on a cutting mat, assuring that the point of the unit faces toward you.

2. Align the diagonal guidelines of the Wing Clipper® with the seams of the Flying Geese unit. You'll automatically be centering the tool over your pieced unit 2 ½" x 4 ½" or 3 ½" x 6 ½" (cutting size).

3. Trim the side and across the top of the Wing Clipper® with your rotary cutter.

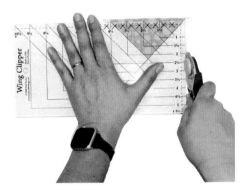

Step 1-3 - Position, Align and Trim

4. Rotate your flying geese unit 180° and reposition the Wing Clipper® to align the previously trimmed raw edge with the 2 ½" x 4 ½" or 3 ½" x 6 ½" and "X" at the top with the intersection of the seams.

5. Trim again, up the side and across the top.

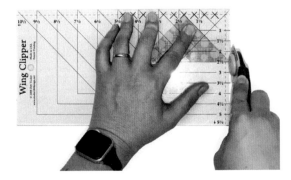

Step 4 -5 - Rotate, Align and Trim

Left-Handed

1. Position the oversize flying geese unit vertically on a cutting mat, assuring that the point of the unit faces toward right.

2. Align the diagonal guidelines of the Wing Clipper® with the seams of the Flying Geese unit. You'll automatically be centering the tool over your pieced unit 2 ½" x 4 ½" or 3 ½" x 6 ½" (cutting size).

3. Trim the left side and across the top of the Wing

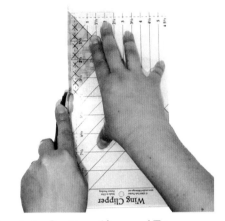

Step 1-3 - Position, Align and Trim

Clipper® with your rotary cutter.

4. Rotate your flying geese unit 180° and reposition the Wing Clipper® to align the previously trimmed raw edge with the 2 ½" x 4 ½" or 3 ½" x 6 ½" and "X" at the top with the intersection of the seams.

5. Trim again, up the left side and across the top.

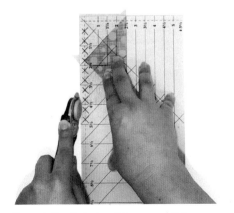

Step 4-5 - Rotate, Align, and Trim

Pickets

Pickets are fundamental unit consist of a rectangle and flipped squares, very similar to the Stitch and Flip Method of making Flying Geese. You can say they are half of a Flying Geese unit. These units will be oversized and will be trimmed down similar to the Flying Geese process.

If you would like more information, pick up the Studio 180 Design Picket & Quickets Technique Sheet.

Process

This method is used in the Petal Spinner project on page 98.

1. Gather one square / one rectangle.

Step 1- Gather

2. Using your Quilter's Magic Wand mark a sewing line from corner to corner diagonally on the wrong side of the square.

3. With right sides facing, Position a square with a rectangle, assuring the center diagonal runs from the bottom left corner to the upper right corner.

Step 2 - 3 - Mark and Position

4. Stitch on the drawn line, then trim ¼" away from sewn line.

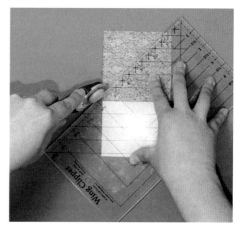

Step 4 - Stitch

5. Press seam toward the triangle.

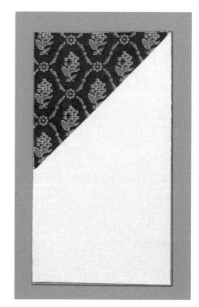

Step 5 - Press

Picket Trimming Down

Right-Handed

1. Position the oversize unit on a cutting mat, assuring the long edge of the rectangle is on the bottom.

2. Position your Wing Clipper® tool over the unit, aligning one of the long diagonal guidelines on the ruler with the single diagonal seam. Assure that the ruler is on the appropriate trim down lines and the lines are inside the oversized unit.

3. Trim up the right side and across the top of the Wing Clipper® with your rotary cutter.

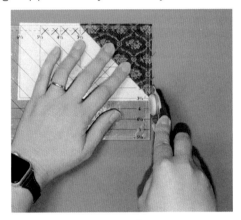

Step 1-3 - Position and Trim

4. Rotate your Picket unit 180° and reposition the Wing Clipper® tool to align the previously trimmed raw edges, the "X" should align with the sewn seam. Trim again, up the right side and across the top.

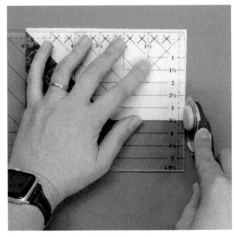

Step 4 - Rotate and Trim

Left-Handed

1. Position the oversize unit on a cutting mat, assuring the long edge of the rectangle is on the right.

2. Position your Wing Clipper® tool over the unit, aligning one of the long diagonal guidelines on the ruler with the single diagonal seam. Assure that the ruler is on the appropriate trim down lines and the lines are inside the oversized unit.

3. Trim up the left side and across the top of the Wing Clipper® with your rotary cutter.

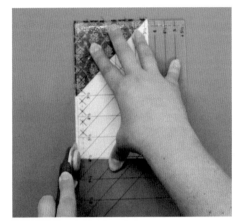

Step 1-3 - Position and Trim

4. Rotate your Picket unit 180° and reposition the Wing Clipper® tool to align the previously trimmed raw edges, the "X" should align with the sewn seam. Trim again, up the left side and across the top.

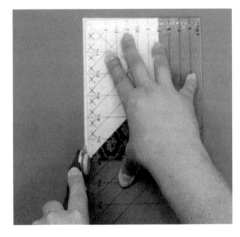

Step 4 - Rotate and Trim

Corner Pop

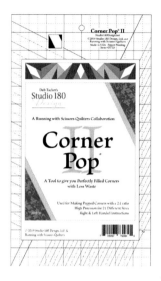

The original Corner Pop® tool was designed to give you perfectly filled corners with less waste by cutting away a 90° corner from a base shape, replacing the corner with a half square triangle. Then by using the tool guidelines to trim up the edges and cleaning up the corners to the perfect size and shape.

In 2019, Deb Tucker's Studio 180 Design released Corner Pop® II and III, a collaboration between Studio 180 Design and Running with Scissors Quilters.

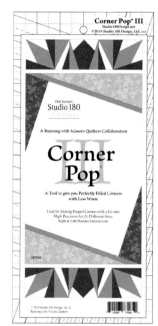

The Corner Pop tools were built upon the same idea of the Original Corner Pop tool to allow you to add perfectly filled corners with less waste. Instead of the 90° corner, the new tools have 2:1 and 3:1 ratio triangles for any base shape.

- Corner Pop® II is designed for a 2:1 ratio corner triangle to any base shape making pops that are twice as high as they are wide.

- Corner Pop® III is designed for a 3:1 ratio corner triangle to any base shape, making pops that are three times as tall as they are wide.

Both tools give you 21 different size options, allowing you to remove any left or right slanting corner by using the tool lines to accurately trim away a corner leaving a ¼" seam allowance. Just like the original Corner Pop® tool, you will follow by adding an oversized Replacement Triangle. Additional guidelines and tool edges allow you to clean up the corner to the perfect final shape and size.

Organization Tip:

It is imperative to be highly organized when you are working on your quilt project. One method I recommend is to use standard cheap paper plates that have no coating. These paper plates are great for storing your units and cut pieces to keep everything organized. Before you start your cutting, mark each paper plate with the unit beginning with the unit name, the number of strips, the number of sub cuts, the unit size, trim size, etc. Please add any additional information that may be helpful to you. This information will help you work through the construction process of each of the quilts. Store your projects, including the fabric on the paper plates, in large Ziplock bags when you need to put them away for a while. Then if you come back to your project months or years down the road, you will have all the information and pieces together to finish the pattern.

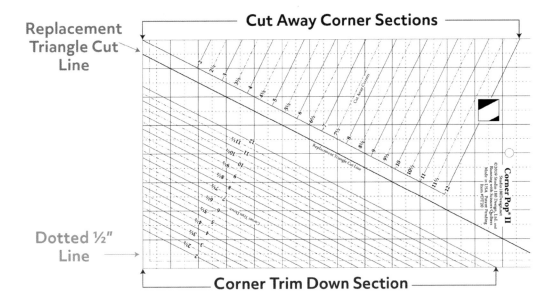

- **Cut Away Corners Section** – The number refers to the finished height of your replaced corner triangle.

- **Corner Trim Down Corner Section** – Align the diagonal lines with the seam lines of your Replacement Triangles to provide accurate cleanup trimming.

- **Replacement Triangle Cut Line** – is the broad diagonal line used on the strips or rectangles for cutting the Replacement Triangles.

- **Dotted ½" line** - can be used in cutting the replacement triangles.

Pressing Tips:

Pressing is a crucial element of assembling your units, blocks, and layouts. To get your units to look crisp and lay flat, I recommend using a hot steam iron. Once your units are pressed, placing a Tailor's Clapper (Clapper Blocks) on the hot seam will help with a little extra pressing as the unit cools.

When working with a lot of bias edges and seams, I recommend using a little mist of Best Press to help hold the shape of the unit. In this book, the pressing direction is indicated by arrows in each project so you can nest the units and blocks together. However, if you prefer to press your seams open, you may do so as well.

Corner Pop II General Instructions

Determine Your Cut Away Type

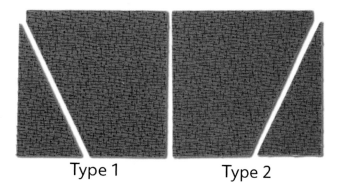

Type 1   **Type 2**

Determine if you are making a Type 1 or Type 2 Cut Away.

- Type 1 – cut on the left and the short side on the bottom.

- Type 2 – cut on the right and the short side on the bottom.

Note: *The base shape can have more than one type of cut away.*

Your finished cut away will depend on the base shape, replacement strip, and finished unit trim orientation.

- **Type 1** (slants from the bottom to left side)

  - Base Shape - placed on cutting mat **Right Side up**.

  - Replacement Triangle - fabric strip will be placed **Right Side up**.

  - Trimming Finished unit - place unit with **Wrong Side up** on cutting mat.

- **Type 2** (slants from the bottom to right side)

  - Base Shape - placed on cutting mat **Wrong Side up**.

  - Replacement Triangle - fabric strip will be placed **Wrong Side up**.

  - Trimming Finished unit - place unit with **Right Side up** on cutting mat.

Corner Pop II Chart of Sizes used in the projects in this book

Finished Cut Away Height	Replacement Triangle Strip Width	Number of Replacement Triangles per WOF	Number of Replacement Triangle Pairs per WOF*
2"	3"	30	15 pairs
3"	4"	24	12 pairs
4"	5"	22	11 pairs

Note: When cutting replacement triangles, you can cut both Type 1 and Type 2 triangles at the same time. This is done by folding the WOF strip in half on the short edge with either right sides facing or wrong sides facing and then following the instruction of the tool for making the cuts. To cut only a Type 1 or a Type 2 you would not fold the WOF strip when making the cuts.

Cutting Replacement Triangles - Type 1

1. Determine the size of the Replacement Triangle Strips based on your project Corner Pop chart. Gather Replacement Triangles strips and clean up the selvage end of the strips.

2. Place a single layer replacement strip **Right Side Up** on your cutting mat.

3. Position the **Replacement Triangle Cut Line** of the Corner Pop® II tool on the trimmed edge of the Replacement Triangle strip and **Cut Away Corner Line** according to your strip width along the long edge of the strip. Cut along the angled edge of the tool.

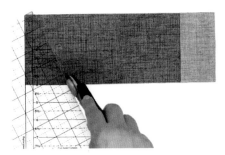

Step 1-3 - Right Handed

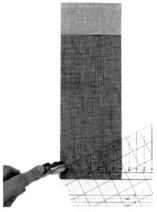

Step 1-3 - Left Handed

4. To make the next cut, position the top edge of the tool on the strip. Position the **½" dashed line** on the tool with the point on the opposite side of the strip. Cut along the straight edge. Repeat to make the number of required Replacement Triangles or Triangle Pairs according to your project.

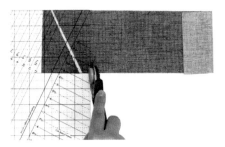

Step 4 - Right Handed

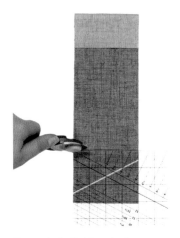

Step 4- Left Handed

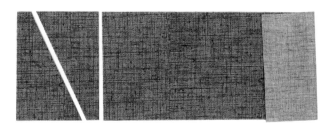

Corner Pop II - Type 1 Replacement Triangles

1. Determine the size of the Replacement Triangle strips based on your project Corner Pop chart, and gather Replacement Triangles strips. Clean up the selvage end of the strip.

2. Place a single layer Replacement strip **Wrong Side Up** on your cutting mat.

3. Position the **Replacement Triangle Cut Line** of the Corner Pop® II tool on the trimmed edge of the Replacement Triangle strip and **Cut Away Corner Line** according to your strip width along the long edge of the strip. Cut along the angled edge of the tool.

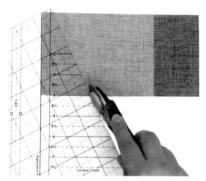

Step 1-3 - Right Handed

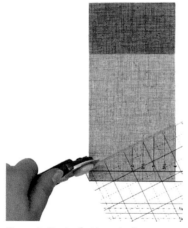

Step 1-3 - Left Handed

4. To make the next cut, position the top edge of the tool on the strip. Position the **½" dashed line** on the tool with the point on the opposite side of the strip. Cut along the straight edge. Repeat to make the number of required Replacement Triangles or Triangle Pairs according to your project.

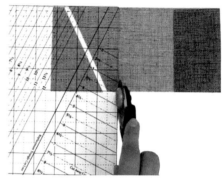

Step 4 - Right Handed

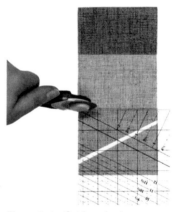

Step 4- Left Handed

Corner Pop II - Type 2 Replacement Triangles

Cut Away Corner - Type 1

1. Gather base shape and Type 1 Replacement Triangles that are used in your project.

Step 1 - Gather

2. Referring to the project Type 1 cutting diagram, place your base shape **Right Side Up** for cutting.

3. Position the Corner Pop® II tool **Cut Away line** over the square, carefully aligning the cut away height according to the project size lines on the tool with the raw edge of the square and trim. Repeat for all base units.

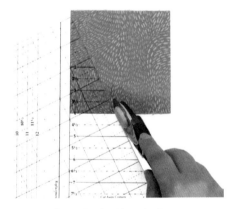

Step 2 & 3 - Right Handed

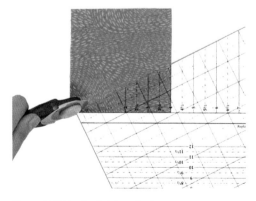

Step 2 & 3 - Left Handed

4. Layout (1) Type 1 Replacement Triangle and (1) base shape. Align the longest diagonal edge of the Replacement Triangle with the newly trimmed edge of the base shape.

Step 4 - Layout

5. Stitch together with the square on top, using an accurate ¼" seam. Repeat to make number of Type 1 units required according to your project instructions.

Step 5 - Stitch

6. Press the seam toward the base unit or open according to your project instructions.

Step 6 - Press

7. Place the finished unit **Wrong Side Up** for trimming. Locate the **Corner Trim Down** section of the Corner Pop® II tool and find the finished size diagonal line. Place the **Corner Trim Down line** on the diagonally sewn seam and line up the cutting edge of the tool with the raw edges of the square. Trim away the excess Replacement Triangle. Repeat to make the required Type 1 units for your project.

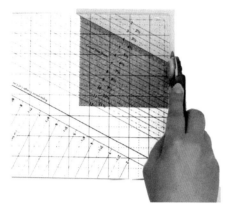

Step 7 - Right Handed

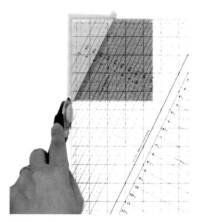

Step 7 - Left Handed

Cut Away Corner - Type 2

1. Gather base shape and Type 2 Replacement Triangles that are used in your project.

2. Referring to the project Type 2 cutting diagram, place your base shape **Wrong Side Up** for cutting.

3. Position the Corner Pop® II tool **Cut Away line** over the square, carefully aligning the cut away height according to the project size lines on the tool with the raw edge of the square and trim. Repeat for all base units.

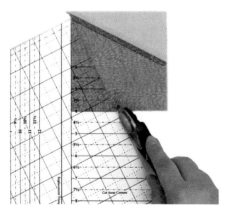

Step 2 & 3 - Right Handed

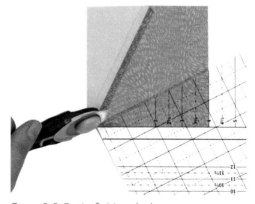

Step 2 & 3 - Left Handed

4. Layout (1) Type 2 Replacement Triangle and (1) base shape. Align the longest diagonal edge of the Replacement Triangle with the newly trimmed edge of the base shape.

Step 4 - Layout

5. Stitch together with the base square on top, using an accurate ¼" seam. Repeat to make the number Type 2 units required for your project.

Step 5 - Stitch

6. Press the seam toward the base unit or open according to your project instructions.

Step 6 - Press

7. Place the finished unit **Right Side Up** for trimming. Locate the **Corner Trim Down** section of the Corner Pop® II tool and find the finished size diagonal line. Place the **Corner Trim Down** line on the diagonally sewn seam and line up the cutting edge of the tool with the raw edges of the square. Trim away the excess Replacement Triangle. Repeat to make correct number of Type 2 units according to your project instructions.

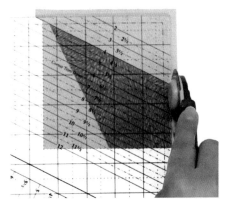

Step 7 - Right Handed

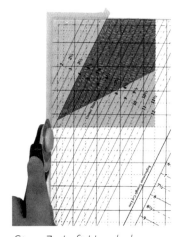

Step 7 - Left Handed

Corner Pop III General Instructions

Determine Your Cut Away Type

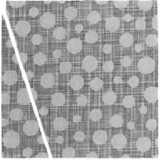
Type 1

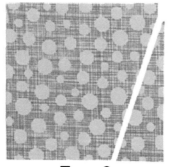
Type 2

Determine the if you are making a Type 1 or Type 2 Cut Away.

- Type 1 – cut on the left and the short side on the bottom.

- Type 2 – cut on the right and the short side on the bottom.

Note: *The base shape can have more than one type of cut away.*

Your finished cut away will depend on the base shape, Replacement Strip, and Finished unit trim orientation.

- **Type 1** (slants from the bottom to left side)

  - Base Shape - placed on your cutting mat **Right Side up.**

  - Replacement Triangle - fabric strip will be placed **Right Side up.**

  - Trimming Finished unit - place unit with **Wrong Side up** on cutting mat.

- **Type 2** (slants from the bottom to right side)

  - Base Shape - placed on cutting mat **Wrong Side up.**

  - Replacement Triangle - fabric strip will be placed **Wrong Side up.**

  - Trimming Finished unit - place unit with **Right Side up** on cutting mat.

Corner Pop III Chart of Sizes used in the projects in this book

Finished Cut Away Height	Replacement Triangle Strip Width	Number of Replacement Triangles per WOF	Number of Replacement Triangle Pairs per WOF*
2"	3"	34	17 pairs
3"	4"	32	16 pairs
4"	5"	26	13 pairs

*Note: When cutting replacement triangles, you can cut both Type 1 and Type 2 triangles at the same time. This is done by folding the WOF strip in half on the short edge with either right sides facing or wrong sides facing and then following the instruction of the tool for making the cuts. To cut only a Type 1 or a Type 2 you would not fold the WOF strip when making the cuts.

Cutting Replacement Triangles - Type 1

1. Determine the size of the Replacement Triangle strips based on your project Corner Pop Chart. Gather Replacement Triangles strips and clean up the selvage end of the strips.

2. Place a single layer Replacement strip **Right Side Up** on your cutting mat.

3. Position the **Replacement Triangle Cut Line** of the Corner Pop® III tool on the trimmed edge of the Replacement Triangle strip and **Cut Away Corner Line** according to your strip width along the long edge of the strip. Cut along the angled edge of the tool.

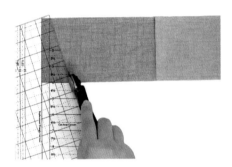

Step 1-3 - Right Handed

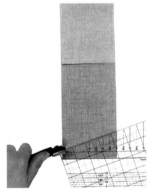

Step 1-3 - Left Handed

4. To make the next cut, position the top edge of the tool on the strip. Position the ½" line on the tool about ⅛" in from the edge of the corner (*see tip below*). Cut along the straight edge. Repeat to make the number of required Replacement Triangles or Triangle Pairs according to your project.

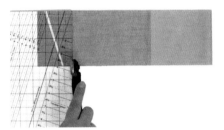

Step 4 - Right Handed

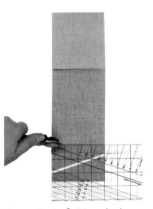

Step 4 - Left Handed

Corner Pop III - Type 1 Replacement Triangle

Marking ToolTips:

To aid in finding the ⅛" every time when making the second replacement triangle cut on the Corner Pop® III, it would be helpful to mark the tool. I recommend using another ruler to find the ⅛" in from the ½" mark on the back of the Corner Pop® III tool, then using a Fine Point Sharpie, mark a line. Alternatively, you could find the ⅛" in from the ½" mark on the top of the Corner Pop® III tool, then mark with a piece of OmniGrip® Glow Line™ Tape.

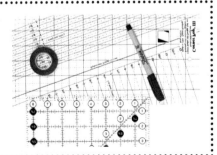

1. Determine the size of the Replacement Triangle Strips based on your project Corner Pop Chart. Gather Replacement Triangles strips and clean up the selvage end of the strips.

2. Place a single layer Replacement strip **Wrong Side Up** on your cutting mat.

3. Position the **Replacement Triangle Cut Line** of the Corner Pop® III tool on the trimmed edge of the Replacement Triangle strip and **Cut Away Corner Line** according to your strip width along the long edge of the strip. Cut along the angled edge of the tool.

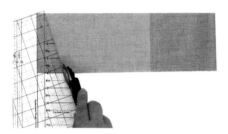

Step 1-3 - Right Handed

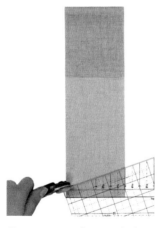

Step 1-3 - Left Handed

4. To make the next cut, position the top edge of the tool on the strip. Position the ½" line on the tool about ⅛" in from the edge of the corner. Cut along the straight edge. Repeat to make the number of required Replacement Triangles or Triangle Pairs according to your project.

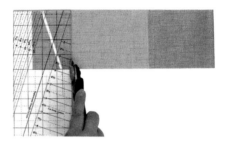

Step 4 - Right Handed

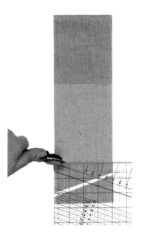

Step 4 - Left Handed

Corner Pop III - Type 2 Replacement Triangle

Cut Away Corner - Type 1

1. Gather base shape and Type 1 Replacement Triangles that are used in your project.

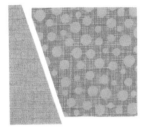

Step 1 - Gather

2. Place your base shape **Right Side Up** for cutting.

3. Position the Corner Pop® III tool **Cut Away line** over the square, carefully aligning the cut away height according to the project size lines on the tool with the raw edge of the square and trim. Repeat for all base units.

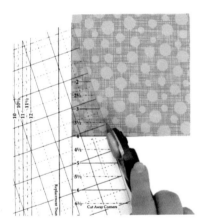

Step 2-3 - Right Handed

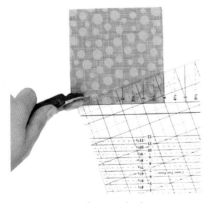

Step 2-3 - Left Handed

4. Layout (1) Type 1 Replacement Triangle and (1) base shape. Align the longest diagonal edge of the Replacement Triangle with the newly trimmed edge of the base unit.

Step 4 - Layout

5. Stitch together with the square on top, using an accurate ¼" seam. Repeat to make the number of Type 1 units required for your project instructions.

Step 5 - Stitch

6. Press the seam toward the Replacement Triangle or open according to your project instructions.

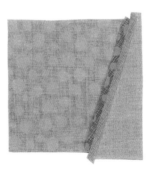

Step 6 - Press

7. Place the finished unit **Wrong Side Up** for trimming. Locate the **Corner Trim Down** section of the Corner Pop® III tool and find the finished size diagonal line. Place the **Corner Trim Down line** on the diagonally sewn seam and line up the cutting edge of the tool with the raw edges of the square. Trim away the excess Replacement Triangle. Repeat to make the required number of Type 1 units for your project.

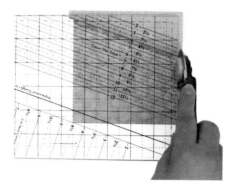

Step 7 - Right Handed

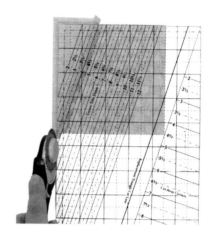

Step 7 - Left Handed

Cut Away Corner - Type 2

1. Gather base shape and Type 2 Replacement Triangles that are used in your project.

2. Place your base shape **Wrong Side Up** for cutting.

3. Position the Corner Pop® III tool **Cut Away line** over the square, carefully aligning the cut away height according to the project size lines on the tool with the raw edge of the square and trim. Repeat for all base units.

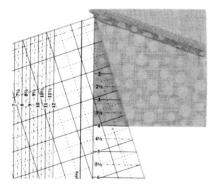

Step 2 & 3 - Right Handed

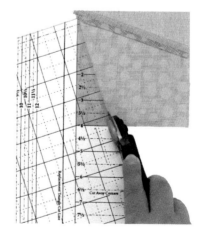

Step 2 & 3 - Left Handed

4. Layout (1) Type 2 Replacement Triangle and (1) base shape. Align the longest diagonal edge of the Replacement Triangle with the newly trimmed edge of the base unit.

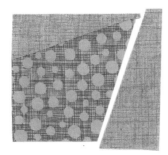

Step 4 - Layout

5. Stitch together with the square on top, using an accurate ¼" seam. Repeat to make the number of Type 2 units according to your project instructions.

Step 5 - Stitch

6. Press the seam toward the replacement triangle or open according to your project instructions.

Step 6 - Press

7. Place the finished unit **Right Side Up** for trimming. Locate the **Corner Trim Down** section of the Corner Pop® III tool and find the finished size diagonal line. Place the Corner Trim Down line on the diagonally sewn seam and line up the cutting edge of the tool with the raw edges of the square. Trim away the excess Replacement Triangle. Repeat to make the make the required number of Type 2 units for your project.

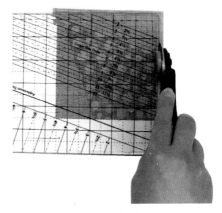

Step 7 - Right Handed

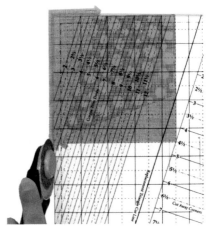

Step 7 - Left Handed

Quilt Center Assembly

Once you have your blocks completed according to the project directions, it is time to assemble them into your quilt top. There are many ways to set your blocks into a quilt. This book uses the Straight and On-Point setting layouts.

Straight layouts are blocks set side by side, edges touching, in vertical and horizontal rows. Examples of projects that use a straight layout setting are Nautical Sails and Mirrored Ombre.

Nautical Sails

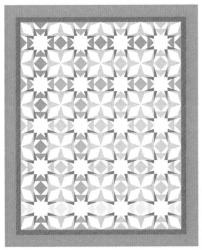
Mirrored Ombre.

Assembly Process for the Straight Layout

Press the quilt project seams as shown in the project diagrams, or press the seams open.

For the Straight Layout, you will assemble your blocks so they will lay side by side to create rows according to the project instructions and diagrams.

1. Lay all the blocks out either on a design board or the floor, as shown in the project layout. This way, you can insure you have every block in the correct position and orientation before sewing.

2. Stitch all the blocks together into rows and press.

3. Stitch the rows together to create your quilt top and press.

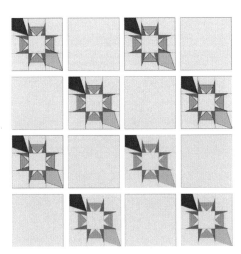
Step 1 - Straight Layout

Step 2 - Stitch Blocks

Step 3 - Stitch Rows

On Point are blocks that are turned 45 degrees, tipping the points of blocks to the cardinal directions, hence the description "on point." Blocks are sewn together in diagonal rows and filled in with side and corner setting triangles to make a square quilt center. Examples of projects that use an on point setting are Asterisk Stars and Echoing Stars.

Asterisk Stars

Echoing Stars

Assembly Process for On Point

Press the quilt project seams as shown in the project diagrams, or press the seams open.

1. Start by cutting your Side and Corner Setting Triangles according to the project instructions.

Step 1 Setting Triangle.   *Step 1 - Corner Triangle*

2. Layout all the blocks either on a design board or the floor, according to the project layout. Arrange the individual diagonal rows and add the side triangles on the ends, as shown in the project layout. This way, you can insure you have every block and triangle in the correct position and orientation before sewing.

Step 2 - On Point layout

3. Stitch all the blocks and Side Triangles into diagonal rows and press.

Step 3 - Stitch Diagonal rows

4. Stitch the diagonal rows together to create your quilt top and press.

5. Finish the assembly by adding the Corner Triangles and press.

6. Square and Trim all the outside edges ¼" to prepare for the borders.

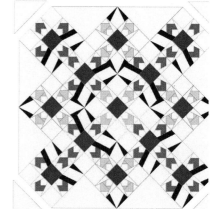

Steps 4 - 5 - Stitch Rows together and add Corner Triangles.

Borders

Borders add a framework for your quilt top to give it a finished look. When it comes to adding the borders and making them lay flat, the correct size is essential. Taking good measurements before you start sewing is the key to stopping your border from waving.

Measure

Start by laying your quilt top out flat on the floor or a table. Measure your quilt top through its center from top to bottom and side to side. If you have a larger quilt top, I suggest taking three different measurements, starting from the outer edges and then down the center from top to bottom. Write these numbers down as you go so you do not have to remember them. You will take these measurements each time before you add a new border to your quilt top.

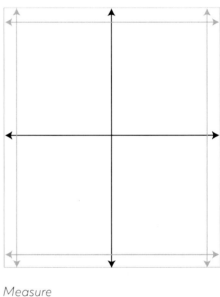

Measure

Join Border Pieces

Depending on the length of your quilt top, you may need to sew two or more strips together to get the correct border length for your quilt top. To avoid wavy borders, it is a good idea to sew the border pieces with a diagonal seam.

Pieced Border

1. Place a border strip end right side up, and place a second border strip right side down overlapping the ends at a 90° angle, allowing a ¼" overhang at the end of each strip.

2. Using a ruler, draw a 45° angle on the top strip, and pin the pieces together.

3. Sew on the drawn line to join the strips together.

4. Trim the excess fabric to leave a ¼" seam allowance and trim the dog ears even to the strip edges.

5. Press the seam open.

6. After joining the number of required border strips together, trim the strip to match the average measured size of the quilt height or width.

Stitching Borders

1. Find and mark the center on the side of your quilt top and the center of your trimmed border strip.

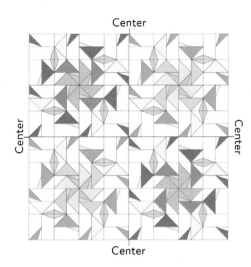

Step 1 - Mark Center

2. Place the marked center of the border strip and the center of the quilt top with the right sides together. Pin the ends of the border strip and the quilt top. Then fill in with as many pins as you need to distribute the fabric evenly.

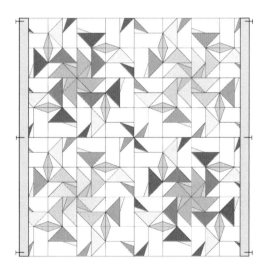

Step 2 - Pin Border Strips

3. Stitch the border to the quilt top using a ¼" seam allowance.

4. Press the seams toward the border strip away from the quilt top.

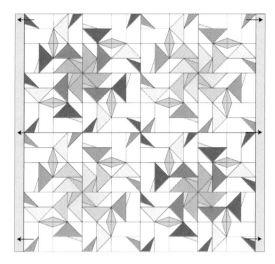

Step 4 - Press

5. Layout your quilt top with the newly added side borders and remeasure across to get the new width of the quilt top. This will be the length of the border strips you need to trim for attaching to the top and bottom of the quilt.

6. Repeat steps 1–4 to add top and bottom border.

Repeat the steps to add all borders that are required to complete your quilt project.

Chapter 4 - Corner Pop II Projects

Asterisk Star
64" x 64"
Page 37

Echoing Stars
65" x 65"
Page 46

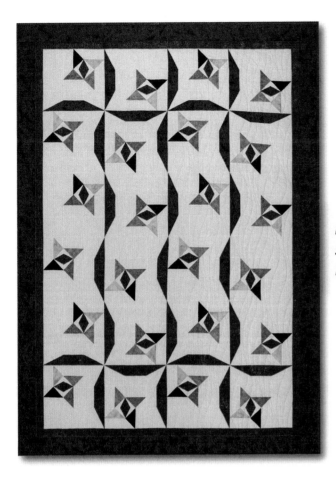

Nautical Sails
58" x 82"
Page 57

Scrappy Spinner
64" x 76"
Page 69

Project 1: Asterisk Star

Finished Block: 12" x 12" · Finished Quilt: 64" x 64"

This elegant quilt top uses the background color to bring out the stencil look in this stunning quilt. The forest colors chosen for this wall hanging add a calming feel that will add a rustic charm to any room.

> Please read through the tool instructions of Corner Pop® II on pages 17-22 for detailed instructions. This will aid you in making the Popped units in this pattern.

Yardage

Based on 40" wide fabric, with an extra strip added for mistakes.

Light Tan – 2 ⅛ yards   Brown – 3 ⅛ yards
Medium Tan – ½ yard   Backing - 4 yards
Green – 1 ⅝ yards   Binding - ⅝ yard

Studio 180 Design Tools

Wing Clipper® I
Corner Pop® II
Quilter's Magic Wand

Unit Summary

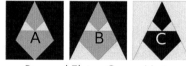

Popped Flying Geese Units
4 ½" Cut Size
(24) Unit A ~ (4) Unit B ~ (24) Unit C

Popped Corner Units
4 ½" Cut Size
(16) Unit D ~ (20) Unit E ~ (16) Unit F

Center Squares
4 ½"
(4) Green ~ (9) Brown

Cutting Chart

Color	Unit	Cut	Subcut		Replacement Triangles	
WOF = Width of Fabric			Squares, Rectangles, Finishing Triangles		Replacement Triangles	
Lt. Tan	Replacement Triangles	4 strips 5" x WOF*			40 Triangle Pairs	
					40 Type 1	40 Type 2
	Popped Corners Base Units	3 strips 4½" x WOF	(20) 4½" squares			
	Flying Geese	7 strips 3" x WOF	(80) 3" squares			
	Border 1	6 strips 2" x WOF				
Med Tan	Flying Geese	2 strips 5½" x WOF	(14) 5½" squares			

Green	Squares	5 strips 4½" x WOF	(36) 4½" squares
			
			Divide into (2) Stacks:
			  (4) Center Squares
			  (32) Popped Corner Base Units			

	Border 3	8 strips 3 ½" x WOF				
Brown	Flying Geese	2 strips 5½" x WOF	(12) 5½" squares			
	Replacement Triangles	6 strips 5" x WOF			64 Triangle Pairs	
					64 Type 1	64 Type 2
	Center Squares	2 strips 4½" x WOF	(9) 4½" squares			
	Flying Geese	2 strips 3" x WOF	(24) 3" squares			
	Corner Setting Triangles	1 strip 9½" x WOF	(2) 9½" squares, cut diagonally once to yield (4) triangles.			
	Side Setting Triangles	1 strip 18½" x WOF	(2) 18½" squares cut diagonally twice to yield (8) triangles.			
	Border 2	7 strips 2½" x WOF				

Flying Geese

Refer to the Flying Geese Instructions on page 8.

Use the listed fabric combinations to make
2 ½" x 4 ½" cut size flying geese.

- (24) 3" Brown / (6) 5 ½" Med. Tan squares - make 24 FG1 units.

- (32) 3" Lt. Tan / (8) 5 ½" Med. Tan squares - make 32 FG2 units.

- (48) 3" Lt. Tan / (12) 5 ½" Brown squares - make 48 FG3 units.

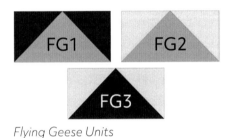

Flying Geese Units

Flying Geese Combination Assembly

Press all the seams according to the diagram.

1. Assemble (1) FG1 and (1) FG2 units as shown. Make (24) 4 ½" Combo1 units.

2. Assemble (2) FG2 units as shown. Make (4) 4 ½" Combo2 units.

3. Assemble (2) FG3 units as shown. Make (24) 4 ½" Combo3 units.

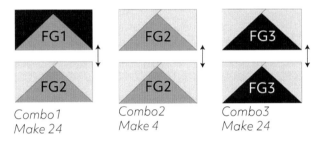

Combo1
Make 24

Combo2
Make 4

Combo3
Make 24

Replacement Triangles

Refer to the Cutting Replacement Triangles for Type 1 and Type 2 on pages 18 and 19.

Use the 5" Cut Away Line to cut a total of

- (64) Brown Type 1 and 2 replacement triangle pairs*.

- (40) Lt. Tan Type 1 and 2 replacement triangle pairs*.

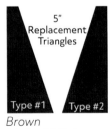

Brown
Make 64 Pairs

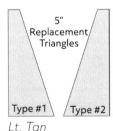

Lt. Tan
Make 40 Pairs

> ***Note:** Separate the Type 1 and 2 Replacement Triangles in two different stacks. I suggest using labeled Paper Plates to help keep yourself organized.*

Popped Flying Geese Units

Refer to the Cut Away Corner Type 1 and 2 on pages 20 and 21. Press seams open.

First Side Pop - Type 1

1. Place combo units **Right Side Up.**

2. Using the **4" Cut Away Line**, trim along the edge of the Combo units as shown.

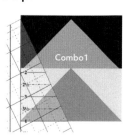

Type 1 Cut Away

3. Referring to the Combo1 diagram below, stitch a 5" Type 1 Replacement Triangle to a Combo base unit. Press seam open.

4. Place the Combo unit **Wrong Side Up**. Trim by using the **4" Corner Trim Down Line** according to the instructions on page 21 - step 7.

5. Make a total of the following :

   - (24) Combo1 / 5" Brown Type 1
   - (4) Combo2 / 5" Brown Type 1
   - (24) Combo3 / 5" Lt. Tan Type 1

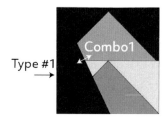

Combo1 - Make 24

*Combo2
Make 4*

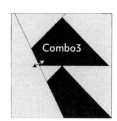

*Combo3
Make 24*

Second Side Pop - Type 2

1. Place combo units **Wrong Side Up**.

2. Using the **4" Cut Away Line**, trim along the edge of the combo unit as shown.

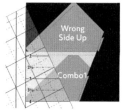

Type 2 Cut Away

3. Referring to Unit A diagram, stitch a 5" Type 2 Replacement Triangle to the combo unit. Press seam open.

4. Place the Combo unit **Right Side Up**. Trim by using the **4" Corner Trim Down Line** according to the instructions on page 22 - step 7.

5. Make a total of the following:

   - (24) Unit A using a Combo 1 / 5" Brown Type 2
   - (4) Unit B using a Combo 2 / 5" Brown Type 2
   - (24) Unit C using a Combo 3 / 5" Lt. Tan Type 2

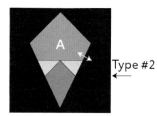

Unit A - Make 24

*Unit B
Make 4*

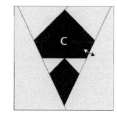

*Unit C
Make 24*

Popped Corner Units

Refer to the Cut Away Corner Type 1 and 2 on pages 20 and 21. Press seams open.

First Side Pop - Type 1

1. Place a 4 ½" base square **Right Side Up.**

2. Using the **4" Cut Away Line**, trim along the edge of the square as shown.

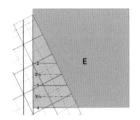

Type 1 Cut Away

3. Referring to the Unit D diagram, stitch a 5" Type 1 Replacement Triangle to the base square. Press seam open.

4. Place the base square **Wrong Side Up.** Trim by using the **4" Corner Trim Down Line** according to the instructions on page 21 - step 7.

5. Make a total of the following:

   • (16) Unit D, using a 4 ½" Green Square / 5" Brown Type 1

   • (20) Unit E, using a 4 ½" Lt. Tan / 5" Brown Type 1

   • (16) Unit F, using a 4 ½" Green Square / 5" Lt. Tan Type 1

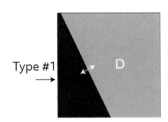

Unit D - Make 16

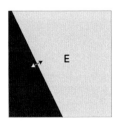

Unit E - Make 20

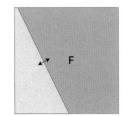

Unit F - Make 16

Second Side Pop - Type 2

1. Place a square **Wrong Side Up**.

2. Using the **4" Cut Away Line**, trim along the edge of the square as shown.

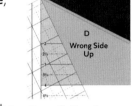

Type 2 Cut Away

3. Referring to the Unit D diagram, stitch a 5" Type 2 Replacement Triangles to the square. Press seam open.

4. Place the square **Right Side Up**. Trim by using the **4" Corner Trim Down Line** according to the instructions on page 22 - step 7.

5. Make a total of the following:

   • (16) Unit D / 5" Brown Type 2

   • (20) Unit E / 5" Brown Type 2

   • (16) Unit F / 5" Lt. Tan Type 2

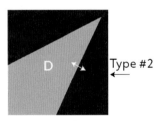

Unit D - Make 16

Unit E - Make 20

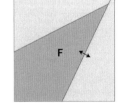

Unit F - Make 16

Block Assembly

1. Lay out the units according to each block layout diagram shown.

2. Stitch the units into rows, pressing seams as shown in the diagram.

3. Stitch the rows together, pressing seams as shown in the diagram.

4. Make the following 12 ½" Blocks.

- (4) Block 1, using (4) Unit D / (4) Unit A / (1) 4 ½" Green Center Square.

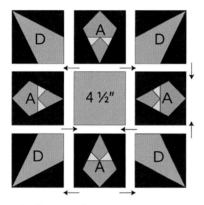

Block 1 - Make 4

- (4) Block 2, using (3) Unit E / (1) Unit F / (2) Unit A / (2) Unit C / (1) 4 ½" Brown Center Square.

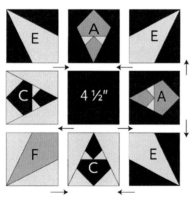

Block 2 - Make 4

- (4) Block 3, using (2) Unit E / (2) Unit F / (1) Unit B / (3) Unit C / (1) 4 ½" Brown Center Square.

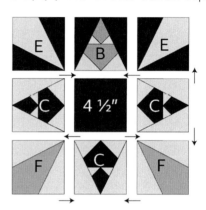

Block 3 - Make 4

- (1) Block 4, using (4) Unit F / (4) Unit C / (1) 4 ½" Brown Center Square.

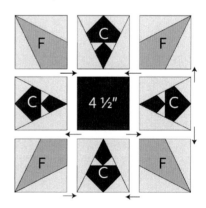

Block 4 - Make 1

Quilt Assembly

1. Lay out the center blocks, side setting triangles, and corner setting triangles as shown in the layout diagram.

2. Stitch the blocks and side setting triangles* into diagonal rows, pressing seams as shown in the diagram.

3. Stitch the rows together to create your quilt top, pressing seams as shown in the diagram, being sure to add the top and bottom corner setting triangles.

4. Trim all outside edges ¼".

> *Note:* The side setting triangles are cut oversized! Carefully match the 90° corners of the setting triangles with the edges of the blocks. The opposite edge will be trimmed later.

5. Using the "Join Border Pieces" detailed instructions on page 32, piece the following together.

Border 1 - Lt. Tan
    Left and Right – Cut (3) strips 2" x WOF. Join together, cut (2) 2" x 51 ½".
    Top and Bottom – Cut (3) strips 2" x WOF. Join together, cut (2) 2" x 54 ½".

Border 2 - Brown
    Left and Right – Cut (3) strips 2 ½" x WOF. Join together, cut (2) 2 ½" x 54 ½".
    Top and Bottom – Cut (4) strips 2 ½" x WOF. Join together, cut (2) 2 ½" x 58 ½".

Border 3 - Green
    Left and Right – Cut (4) strips 3 ½" x WOF. Join together, cut (2) 3 ½" x 58 ½".
    Top and Bottom – Cut (4) strips 3 ½" x WOF. Join together, cut (2) 3 ½" x 64 ½".

6. Stitch Borders 1, 2, and 3 according to the detailed instructions on page 33. Press according to the quilt layout on page 45.

Finishing

Layer, quilt, and bind as desired.

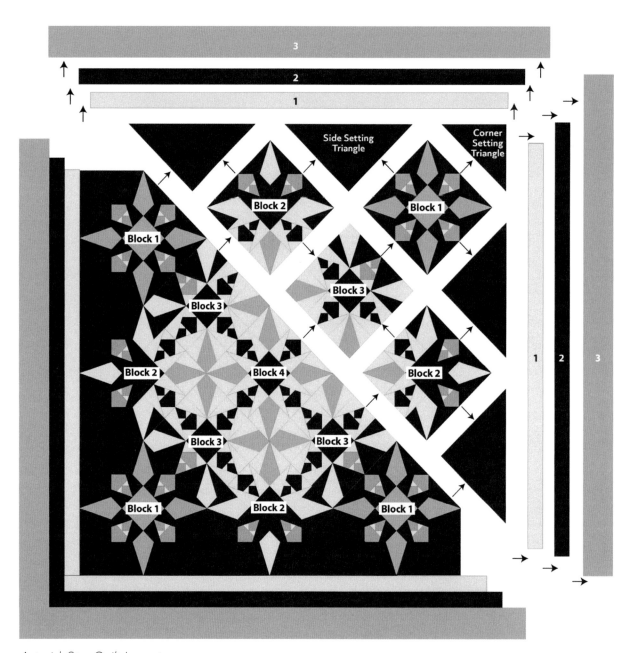

Asterisk Star Quilt Layout

Project 2: Echoing Stars

Finished Block: 12" x 12" · Finished Quilt: 65" x 65"

Shapes inside of shapes add a lot of fun to this wall hanging quilt. The different star shapes throughout make circles and an "X" keeps your eyes diving deeper into the design. It is an enjoyable quilt that is suitable for many different color palettes. The fabrics chosen for this quilt bring both warm and cool colors together to add balance.

Please read through the tool instructions of Corner Pop® II on pages 17-22 for detailed instructions. This will aid you in making the Popped units in this pattern.

Yardage

Based on 40" wide fabric, with an extra strip added for mistakes.

Background – 2 ⅛ yards

Light Pink – ½ yard

Dark Pink – ¾ yard

Green – 1 ⅛ yards

Gray – ¾ yard

Dark Blue – 1 ⅜ yards

Black – ¾ yard

Backing - 4 ⅛ yards

Binding - ⅝ yard

Studio 180 Design Tools

Wing Clipper® I

Corner Pop® II

Quilter's Magic Wand

Unit Summary

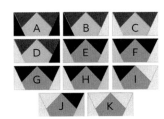

Popped Flying Geese Units

2 ½" x 4 ½" Cut Size

(36) Unit A ~ (4) Unit B ~ (8) Unit C
(4) Unit D ~ (8) Unit E ~ (4) Unit F
(20) Unit G ~ (4) Unit F ~ (4) Unit H
(4) Unit I ~ (8) Unit J

Popped Corner Units

4 ½" Cut Size

(16) Unit L ~ (8) Unit M

Center Squares

4 ½"

(36) Background ~ (5) Gray

Cutting Chart

Color	Unit	Cut	Subcut	
			Squares, Rectangles, Finishing Triangles	Replacement Triangles
WOF = Width of Fabric				
Background	Replacement Triangles	1 strip 5" x WOF*		8 Triangle Pairs
				8 Type 1 · 8 Type 2
	Center Squares	5 strips 4½" x WOF	(36) 4½" squares	
	Flying Geese	1 strip 3" x WOF	(12) 3" squares	
	Replacement Triangles	2 strips 3" x WOF		48 Triangle Pairs
				48 Type 1 · 48 Type 2
	Corner Setting Triangles	1 strip 9½" x WOF	(2) 9½" squares, cut diagonally once to yield (4) triangles.	
	Side Setting Triangles	1 strip 18½" x WOF	(2) 18½" squares, cut diagonally twice, to yield (8) triangles.	
Light Pink	Flying Geese	2 strips 5½" x WOF	(13) 5½" squares	
Dark Pink	Flying Geese	4 strips 3" x WOF	(52) 3" squares	
	Border 1	6 strips 2" x WOF		
Green	Flying Geese	2 strips 5½" x WOF	(13) 5½" squares	
	Border 2	7 strips 3" x WOF		
Gray	Replacement Triangles	2 strips 5" x WOF		16 Triangle Pairs
				16 Type 1 · 16 Type 2
	Center Squares	1 strip 4½" x WOF	(5) 4½" squares	
	Replacement Triangles	1 strip 3" x WOF		16 Triangle Pairs
				16 Type 1 · 16 Type 2
Dark Blue	Popped Corner Base Units	3 strips 4½" x WOF	(24) 4½ squares	
	Border 3	8 strips 3½" x WOF		
Black	Flying Geese	4 strips 3" x WOF	(40) 3" squares	
	Replacement Triangles	3 strips 3" x WOF		40 Triangle Pairs
				40 Type 1 · 40 Type 2

Flying Geese

Refer to the Flying Geese Instructions on page 8.

Use the listed fabric combinations to make 2 ½" x 4 ½" cut size flying geese.

- (52) 3" Dark Pink / (13) 5 ½" Light Pink squares - make 52 FG1 Units.

- (36) 3" Black / (9) 5 ½" Green squares - make 36 FG2 Units.

- (4) 3" Black / (2) 5 ½" Green / (4) 3" Background squares - make 8 FG Units, divided in half (4) FG3 and (4) FG4 units*.

- (8) 3" Background / (2) 5 ½" Green squares - make 8 FG5 Units.

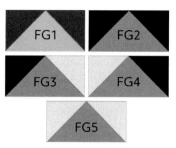

Flying Geese Units

> ***Note:*** For FG3 and FG4, start with stitching the (2) Black 3" squares on the 5 ½" green square. Then follow up with the (2) 3" Background squares to make the partial FG units.

Replacement Triangles

Refer to the Cutting Replacement Triangles for Type 1 and Type 2 on pages 18 and 19.

1. Use the 3" Cut Away Line for the 3" to cut a total of

   - (48) 3" Background Type 1 and 2 replacement triangle pairs**.

   - (16) 3" Gray Type 1 and 2 replacement triangles pairs**.

   - (40) 3" Black Type 1 and 2 replacement triangles pairs**.

> ** **Note:** Separate the Type 1 and 2 Replacement Triangles in two different stacks. I suggest using labeled Paper Plates to help keep yourself organized.

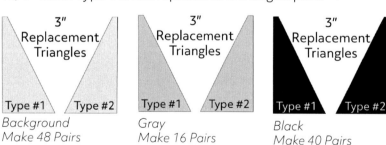

Background Make 48 Pairs   *Gray Make 16 Pairs*   *Black Make 40 Pairs*

2. Use the 5" Cut Away Line for the 5" to cut a total of

   - (8) 5" Background replacement triangles pairs**.

   - (16) 5" Gray replacement triangles pairs**.

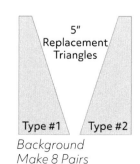
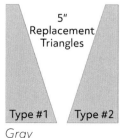

Background Make 8 Pairs   *Gray Make 16 Pairs*

Popped Flying Geese

Refer to the Cut Away Corner Type 1 on page 20. Press seams open.

First Side Pop - Type 1

1. Place a FG base unit **Right Side Up**.

2. Using the **2" Cut Away Line,** trim along the edge of the FG unit as shown below.

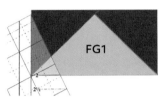

Type 1 Cut Away

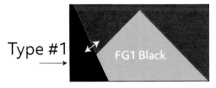

FG1 Black - Make 40

3. Referring to the FG1 Black diagram to the right, stitch a 3" Type 1 Replacement Triangle to the FG base unit. Press seam open.

4. Place the FG unit **Wrong Side Up**. Trim by using the **2" Corner Trim Down Line** according to the instructions on page 21- step 7.

5. Make a total of the following:

   - (40) FG1 / 3" Black Type 1

   - (12) FG1/ 3" Background Type 1

   - (12) FG2 / 3" Gray Type 1

   - (24) FG2 / 3" Background Type 1

   - (4) FG3 / 3" Gray Type 1

   - (4) FG4 / 3" Background Type 1

   - (8) FG5 / 3" Background Type 1

*FG1 Background
Make 12*

*FG2 Gray
Make 12*

*FG2 Background
Make 24*

FG3 Gray - Make 4

*FG4 Background
Make 4*

*FG5 Background
Make 8*

Popped Flying Geese

Refer to the Cut Away Corner Type 2 on page 21. Press seams open.

Second Side Pop - Type 2

1. Place a FG unit **Wrong Side Up**.

2. Using the **2" Cut Away Line,** trim along the edge of the FG unit as shown.

Type 2 Cut Away

3. Referring to the Unit A diagram to the right, stitch a 3" Type 2 Replacement Triangle to the FG unit. Press seams open.

4. Place the FG unit **Right Side Up**. Trim by using the **2" Corner Trim Down Line** according to the instructions on page 22- step 7.

5. Make a total of the following:

   - (36) Unit A using a FG1 Black / 3" Black Type 2

   - (4) Unit B using a FG1 Black / 3" Background Type 2

   - (8) Unit C using a FG1 Background / 3" Background Type 2

   - (4) Unit D using a FG1 Background / 3" Black Type 2

   - (8) Unit E using a FG2 Gray / 3" Gray Type 2

   - (4) Unit F using a FG2 Gray / 3" Background Type 2

   - (20) Unit G using a FG2 Background / 3" Background Type 2

   - (4) Unit H using a FG2 Background / 3" Gray Type 2

   - (4) Unit I using a FG3 Gray / 3" Background Type 2

   - (4) Unit J using a FG4 Background / 3" Gray Type 2

   - (8) Unit K using a FG5 background / 3" Background Type 2

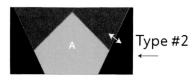

Unit A - Make 36

Unit B - Make 4

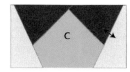

Unit C - Make 8

Unit D - Make 4

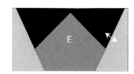

Unit E - Make 8

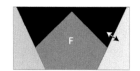

Unit F - Make 4

Unit G - Make 20

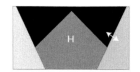

Unit H - Make 4

Unit I - Make 4

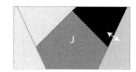

Unit J - Make 4

Unit K - Make 8

Flying Geese Combination Unit

Press seams as shown in the diagram.

1. Assemble (20) Unit G and (20) Unit A as shown. Make (20) 4 ½" Combo1 units.

2. Assemble (4) Unit I and (4) Unit B as shown. Make (4) 4 ½" Combo2 units.

3. Assemble (4) Unit J and (4) Unit D as shown. Make (4) 4 ½" Combo3 units.

4. Assemble (8) Unit K and (8) Unit C as shown. Make (8) 4 ½" Combo4 units.

5. Assemble (4) Unit H and (4) Unit A as shown. Make (4) 4 ½" Combo5 units.

6. Assemble (4) Unit F and (4) Unit A as shown. Make (4) 4 ½" Combo6 units.

7. Assemble (8) Unit E and (8) Unit A as shown. Make (8) 4 ½" Combo7 units.

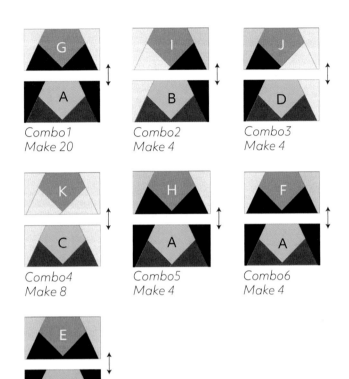

Combo1
Make 20

Combo2
Make 4

Combo3
Make 4

Combo4
Make 8

Combo5
Make 4

Combo6
Make 4

Combo7
Make 8

Popped Corner

Refer to the Cut Away Corner Type 1 and 2 on pages 20 and 21. Press seams open.

First Side Pop - Type 1

1. Place a 4 ½" base square **Right Side Up**.

2. Using the **4" Cut Away Line**, trim along the edge of the square as shown below.

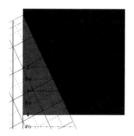

Type 1 Cut Away

3. Referring to the Unit L diagram below, stitch a 5" Type 1 Replacement Triangle to the base square. Press the seam open.

4. Place the base square unit **Wrong Side Up**. Trim by using the **4" Corner Trim Down Line** according to the instructions on page 21 - step 7.

5. Make a total of the following:

   - (16) Unit L, using a 4 ½" Dark Blue squares / 5" Gray Type 1.

   - (8) Unit M, using a 4 ½" Dark Blue squares / 5" Background Type 1.

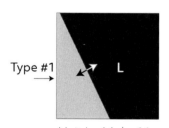

Unit L - Make 16

Unit M - Make 8

Second Side Pop - Type 2

1. Place a square unit **Wrong Side Up**.

2. Using the **4" Cut Away Line**, trim along the edges of the square as shown.

Type 2 Cut Away

3. Referring to the Unit L diagram below, stitch a 5" Type 2 Replacement Triangle to a square. Press seam open.

4. Place the square **Right Side Up**. Trim by using the **4" Corner Trim Down Line** according to the instructions on page 22 - step 7.

5. Make a total of the following:

   - (16) Unit L / 5" Gray Type 2

   - (8) Unit M / 5" Background Type 2

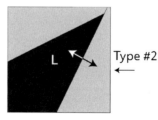

Unit L - Make 16

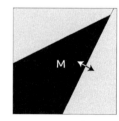

Unit M - Make 8

Block Assembly

1. Lay out the units according to each block layout diagram shown.

2. Stitch the units into rows, pressing seams as shown in the diagram.

3. Stitch the rows together, pressing seams as shown in the diagram .

4. Make the following 12 ½" Blocks:

- (4) Block 1 using (4) Combo 1 units / (5) 4 ½" background squares units.

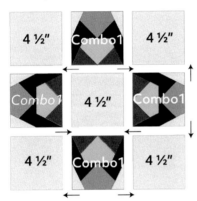

Block1 - Make 4

- (4) Block 2 using (2) Combo4 / (1) Combo2 / (1) Combo 3 / (1) Unit L / (4) 4 ½" Background squares.

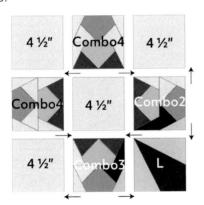

Block2 - Make 4

- (4) Block 3 using (1) Combo5 / (1) Combo7 / (1) Combo1 / (1) Combo6 / (2) Unit L / (2) Unit M / (1) 4 ½" Gray square.

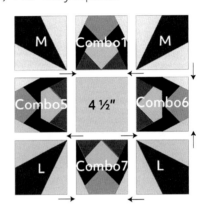

Block3 - Make 4

- (1) Block 4 using (4) Combo7 / (4) Unit L / (1) 4 ½" Gray square.

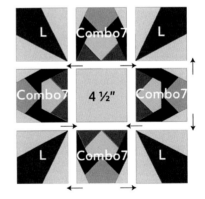

Block4 - Make 1

Quilt Assembly

1. Lay out the center blocks, side setting triangles, and corner setting triangles as shown in the layout diagram.

2. Stitch the blocks and side setting triangles* into diagonal rows, pressing seams as shown in the diagram.

3. Stitch the rows together to create your quilt top, pressing seams as shown in the diagram, being sure to add the top and bottom corner setting triangles.

4. Trim all outside edges ¼".

> *Note:* The side setting triangles are cut oversized! Carefully match the 90° corners of the setting triangles with the edges of the blocks. The opposite edge will be trimmed later.

5. Using the "Join Border Pieces" detailed instructions on page 32, piece the following together:

   Border 1 – Dark Pink
       Left and Right – Cut 3 strips 2" x WOF. Join together, cut (2) 2" x 51 ½"
       Top and Bottom – Cut 3 strips 2" x WOF. Join together, cut (2) 2" x 54 ½"

   Border 2 – Green
       Left and Right – Cut 3 strips 3" x WOF. Join together, cut (2) 3" x 54"
       Top and Bottom – Cut 4 strips 3" x WOF. Join together, cut (2) 3" x 59 ½"

   Border 3 – Dark Blue
       Left and Right – Cut 4 strips 3 ½" x WOF. Join together, cut (2) 3 ½" x 59 ½"
       Top and Bottom – Cut 4 strips 3 ½" x WOF. Join together, cut (2) 3 ½" x 65 ½"

6. Stitch Borders 1, 2 and 3 according to the detailed instructions on page 33. Press according to the quilt layout on page 56.

Finishing

Layer, quilt, and bind as desired

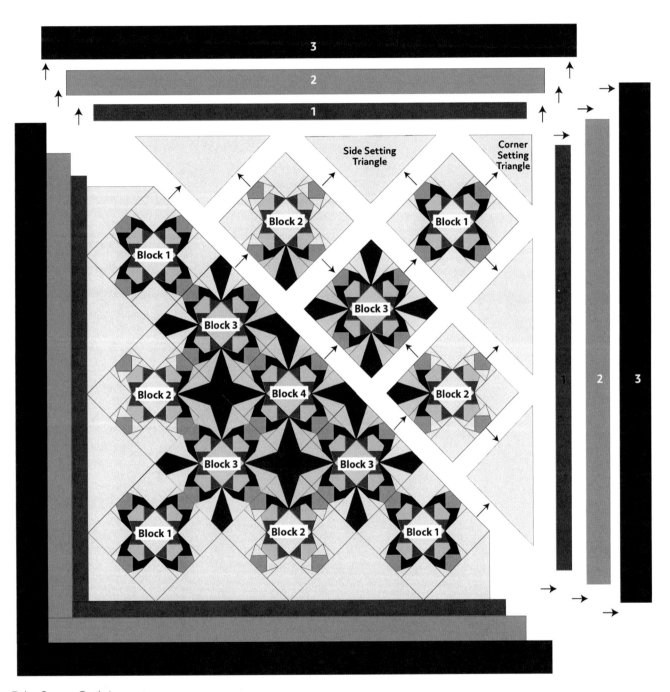

Echo Starts Quilt Layout

Project 3: Nautical Sails

Finished Block: 12" x 12" · Finished Quilt: 58" x 82"

Nautical Sails was inspired by the joy and freedom of sailing over the open water. The shapes in this lovely quilt give the feel of the wind over a lake or ocean—an easy to put together lap size quilt that will warm any sailor's heart.

> Please read through the tool instructions of Corner Pop® II on pages 17-22 for detailed instructions. This will aid you in making the Popped units in this pattern.

Yardage

Based on 40" wide fabric, with an extra strip added for mistakes.

Assorted Light and Medium Blue – 1 Fat Quarter each (4 total)

Background – 3 ⅜ yards

Blue – 1 ½ yards

Red – 1 ⅜ yards

Backing - 5 yards

Binding - ⅝ yard

Studio 180 Design Tools

Wing Clipper® I

Corner Pop® II

Quilter's Magic Wand

Unit Summary

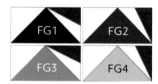

Popped Flying Geese Units
2 ½" x 4 ½" Cut Size
(24) FG1 ~ (24) FG2
(24) FG3 ~ (24) FG4

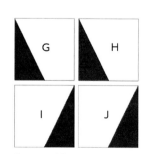

Popped Squares Units
4 ½" Cut Size
(11) Unit G ~ (11) Unit H
(11) Unit I ~ (11) Unit J

Popped Corner Units
4 ½" Cut Size
(2) Unit K ~ (2) Unit L

Rectangles
2½" x 4 ½"
(122) Background ~
(13) Blue ~ (13) Red

Squares
4 ½"
(94) Background

Cutting Chart

Color	Unit	Cut	Squares, Rectangles, Finishing Triangles	Replacement Triangles	
*WOF = Width of Fabric					
Assorted Light and Medium Blues	Flying Geese	2 strips 5½" x 20"	(Cut from each fabric) (6) 5½" squares, total of 24 squares		
Background	Squares	12 strips 4½" x WOF*	(94) 4½" squares, divided into (3) Stacks: (46) Squares (44) Popped Squares (4) Popped Corner		
	Rectangles	8 strips 4½" x WOF	(122) 2½" x 4½" rectangles		
	Flying Geese	8 strips 3" x WOF	(96) 3" squares		
Blue	Replacement Triangles	2 strips 5" x WOF		13 Triangle Pairs	
				13 Type 1	13 Type 2
	Rectangles	1 strip 4½" x WOF	(13) 2½" x 4½" rectangles		
	Border 2	8 strips 4" x WOF			
Red	Replacement Triangles	2 strips 5" x WOF		13 Triangle Pairs	
				13 Type 1	13 Type 2
	Rectangles	1 strip 4½" x WOF	(13) 2½" x 4½" rectangles		
	Replacement Triangles	4 strips 3" x WOF		48 Triangle Pairs	
				48 Type 1	48 Type 2
	Border 1	7 strips 2" x WOF			

Flying Geese

Refer to the Flying Geese Instructions on page 8.

1. Using the following fabric combinations to make 2 ½" x 4 ½" cut size flying geese units.

   - (96) 3" White squares / (24) 5 ½" Assorted Blue squares - make 96 FG Units.

2. Sort the (96) FG Units by color into four stacks of 24 and label them FG1, FG2, FG3, FG4.

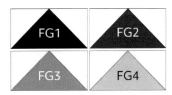

Flying Geese Units

Replacement Triangles

Refer to the Cutting Replacement Triangles for Type 1 and 2 on pages 18 and 19.

1. Use the 5" Cut Away Line for the 5" strips to cut a total of

   - (13) Blue Type 1 and 2 replacement triangle pairs*.

   - (13) Red Type 1 and 2 replacement triangles pairs*.

2. Use the 3" Cut Away Line for the 3" strips to cut a total of

   - (48) 3" Red Type 1 and 2 replacement triangles pairs*.

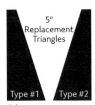
Blue
Make 13 Pairs

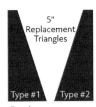
Red
Make 13 Pairs

Red
Make 48 Pairs

> ***Note:*** Separate the Type 1 and 2 Replacement Triangles in two different stacks. I suggest using labeled Paper Plates to help keep yourself organized.

Popped Flying Geese

Refer to the Cut Away Corner Type 1 and 2 on pages 20 and 21. Press seams open.

First Side Pop - Type 1

1. Place a FG unit **Right Side Up**.

2. Using the **2" Cut Away Line,** trim along the edge of the FG base unit as shown below.

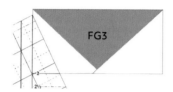

Type 1 Cut Away

3. Referring to the FG3 diagram below, stitch a 3" Red Type 1 Replacement Triangle to a FG base unit. Press seam open.

4. Place the FG unit **Wrong Side Up**. Trim by using the **2" Corner Trim Down Line** according to the instructions on page 21 - step 7.

5. Make a total of the following:

   - (24) FG3 / 3" Red Type 1

   - (24) FG4 / 3" Red Type 1

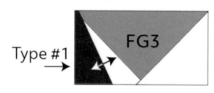

FG3 - Make 24

FG4 - Make 24

First Side Pop - Type 2

1. Place a FG unit **Wrong Side Up**.

2. Using the **2" Cut Away Line**, trim along the edge of the FG base unit as shown below.

Type 2 Cut Away

3. Referring to the FG1 diagram below, stitch a 3" Red Type 2 Replacement Triangle to a FG base unit. Press seam open.

4. Place the FG unit **Right Side Up**. Trim by using the **2" Corner Trim Down Line** according to the instructions on page 22 - step 7.

5. Make a total of the following:

   - (24) FG1 / 3" Red Type 2

   - (24) FG2 / 3" Red Type 2

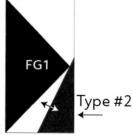

FG1 - Make 24

FG2 Make 24

Combination Units

Press as shown in the diagram.

Assemble the following combination units as shown.

- (24) Unit A, using a FG1 / 2 ½" x 4 ½" Background Rectangle
- (24) Unit B, using a FG2 / 2 ½" x 4 ½" Background Rectangle
- (24) Unit C, using a FG3 / 2 ½" x 4 ½" Background Rectangle
- (24) Unit D, using a FG4 / 2 ½" x 4 ½" Background Rectangle
- (13) Unit E, using a 2 ½" x 4 ½" Background Rectangle / 2 ½" x 4 ½" Red Rectangle
- (13) Unit F, using a 2 ½" x 4 ½" Background Rectangle / 2 ½" x 4 ½" Blue Rectangle

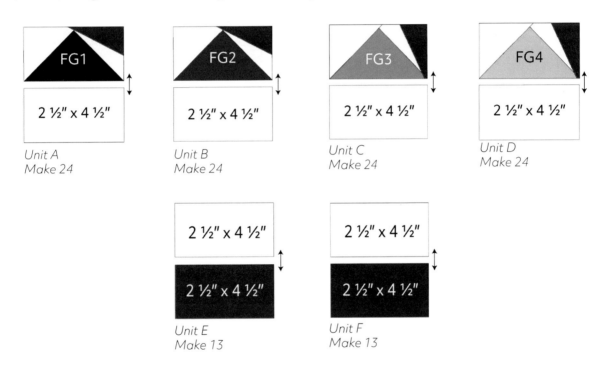

Unit A
Make 24

Unit B
Make 24

Unit C
Make 24

Unit D
Make 24

Unit E
Make 13

Unit F
Make 13

Popped Square Units

Refer to the Cut Away Corner Type 1 and 2 on pages 20 and 21. Press seams open.

First Side Pop - Type 1

1. Place a 4 ½" base square **Right Side Up**.

2. Using the **4" Cut Away Line**, trim along the edge of the base square as shown.

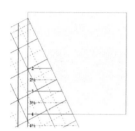

Type 1 Cut Away

3. Referring to the Unit G diagram below, stitch a 5" Type 1 Replacement Triangle to a base square. Press seam open.

4. Place the square unit **Wrong Side Up**. Trim by using the **4" Corner Trim Down Line** according to the instructions on page 21 - step 7.

5. Make a total of the following:

   • (11) Unit G, using a 4 ½" Background square / 5" Blue Type 1

   • (11) Unit H using a 4 ½" Background square / 5" Red Type 1

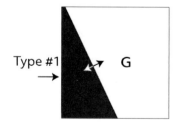

Unit G - Make 11

Unit H - Make 11

First Side Pop - Type 2

1. Place a 4 ½" base square **Wrong Side Up**.

2. Using the **4" Cut Away Line**, trim along the edge of the base square as shown.

Type 2 Cut Away

3. Referring to the Unit I diagram below, stitch a 5" Type 2 Replacement Triangle to a base square. Press seam open.

4. Place the base square unit **Right Side Up**. Trim by using the **4" Corner Trim Down Line** according to the instructions on page 22 - step 7.

5. Make a total of the following:

   • (11) Unit I / 5" Blue Type 2

   • (11) Unit J / 5" Red Type 2

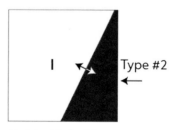

Unit I - Make 11

Unit J - Make 11

Popped Corner

Refer to the Cut Away Corner Type 1 and 2 on pages 20 and 21. Press seams open.

First Side Pop - Type 1

1. Place a 4 ½" base square **Right Side Up**.

2. Using the **4" Cut Away Line,** trim along the edge of the base square as shown.

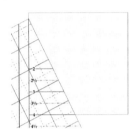

Type 1 Cut Away

3. Referring to the Unit K diagram below, stitch a 5" Type 1 Replacement Triangle to a base square. Press seam open.

4. Place the square unit **Wrong Side Up**. Trim by using the **4" Corner Trim Down Line** according to the instructions on page 21 - step 7.

5. Make a total of the following:

   - (2) Unit K, using a 4 ½" Background square / 5" Blue Type 1

   - (2) Unit L, using a 4 ½" Background square / 5" Red Type 1

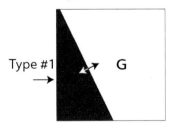

Unit K - Make 2

Unit L - Make 2

Second Side Pop - Type 2

1. Place a square **Wrong Side Up**.

2. Using the **4" Cut Away Line**, trim on the edge of the square as shown.

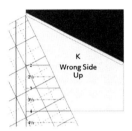

Type 2 Cut Away

3. Refer to the Unit K diagram, stitch a 5" Type 2 Replacement Triangle to a square. Press seam open.

4. Place the square unit **Right Side Up**. Trim by using the **4" Corner Trim Down Line** according to the instructions on page 22 - step 7.

5. Make a total of the following:

   - (2) Unit K / 5" Blue Type 2

   - (2) Unit L / 5" Red Type 2

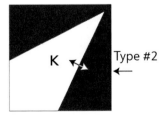

Unit K- Make 2

Unit L - Make 2

Block Assembly

1. Lay out the units according to each block layout diagram shown.

2. Stitch the units into rows, pressing seams as shown as shown in the diagram.

3. Stitch the rows together, pressing seams as shown in the diagram.

4. Make the following 12 ½" Blocks.

- (8) Block 1, using (1) Unit A / (1) Unit B / (1) Unit C / (1) Unit D / (1) Unit G / (1) Unit I / (1) Unit F / (2) 4 ½" squares.

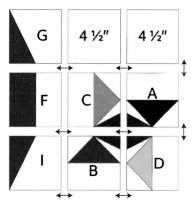

Block 1 - Make 8

- (8) Block 2, using (1) Unit A / (1) Unit B / (1) Unit C / (1) Unit D / (1) Unit H / (1) Unit J / (1) Unit E / (2) 4 ½" squares.

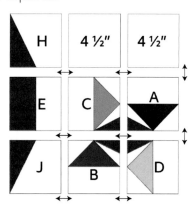

Block 2 - Make 8

- (1) Block 3, using a (1) Unit A / (1) Unit B / (1) Unit C / (1) Unit D / (1) Unit G / (1) Unit I / (1) Unit F / (2) 4 ½" squares.

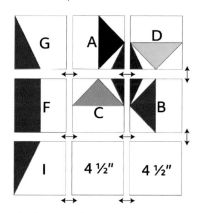

Block 3 - Make 1

- (1) Block 4, using a (1) Unit A / (1) Unit B / (1) Unit C / (1) Unit D / (1) Unit H / (1) Unit J / (1) Unit E / (2) 4 ½" squares.

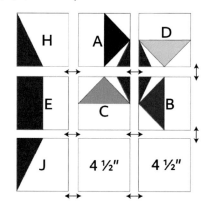

Block 4 - Make 1

- (2) Block 5, using a (1) Unit A / (1) Unit B / (1) Unit C / (1) Unit D / (1) Unit G / (1) Unit I / (2) Unit F / (1) Unit K.

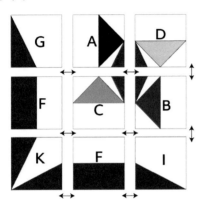

Block 5 - Make 2

- (2) Block 6, using a (1) Unit A / (1) Unit B / (1) Unit C / (1) Unit D / (1) Unit H / (1) Unit J / (2) Unit E / (1) Unit L.

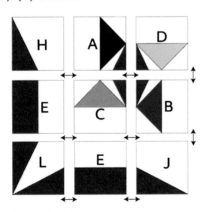

Block 6 - Make 2

- (2) Block 7, using a (1) Unit A / (1) Unit B / (1) Unit C / (1) Unit D / (5) 4 ½" squares.

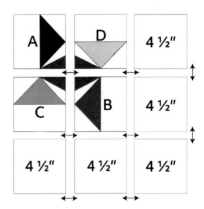

Block 7 - Make 2

Quilt Assembly

1. Lay out the 12 ½" blocks as shown in the layout diagram.

2. Stitch the blocks into horizontal rows, and press as indicated in the diagram.

3. Stitch the rows together to create your quilt top, pressing as shown in the diagram.

4. Using the "Join Border Pieces" detailed instructions on page 32, piece the following together:

    Border 1 - Red
    Left and Right – Cut 4 strips 2" x WOF. Join together, cut (2) 2" x 72 ½"
    Top and Bottom – Cut 3 strips 2" x WOF. Join together, cut (2) 2" x 51 ½"

    Border 2 – Blue
    Left and Right – Cut 4 strips 4" x WOF. Join together, cut (2) 4" x 75 ½"
    Top and Bottom – Cut 4 strips 4" x WOF. Join together, cut (2) 4" x 58 ½"

5. Stitch Border 1 and 2 according to the detailed instructions on page 33. Press according to the quilt layout on page 68.

Finishing

Layer, quilt, and bind as desired.

Nautical Sails Quilt Layout

Project 4: Scrappy Spinner
Finished Block: 12" x 12" · Finish Quilt: 64" x 76"

Scrappy Spinner is a quilt designed to break out the scrap bin and have fun playing with all the leftover fabrics from other projects. This lap-sized quilt can use just a few or many different colors; it just depends on what is in your stash. Relax, have fun with colors, and take your scraps to a whole new level as you make spinning elements and diamonds in this entertaining quilt top.

> Please read through the tool instructions of Corner Pop® II on pages 17-22 for detailed instructions. This will aid you in making the Popped units in this pattern.

Yardage

Based on 40" wide fabric, with an extra strip added for mistakes.

Assorted Medium and Darks - ½ yard each (4 total)

Background – 4 yards

Tan – 1 ½ yards

Light Gray – 1 ⅛ yards

Backing - 4 ¾ yards

Binding - ⅝ yard

Studio 180 Designs Tools

Wing Clipper® I

Corner Pop® II

Quilter's Magic Wand

Unit Summary

Popped Flying Geese Units
3 ½" x 6 ½" Cut Size
(80) Assorted

Popped Rectangle Units
3 ½" x 6 ½" Cut Size
(40) Unit A ~ (18) Unit B ~ (40) Unit C ~ (18) Unit D

Popped Square Units
3 ½" Cut Size
(4) Unit E

Cutting Chart

Color	Unit	Cut	Subcut	
			Squares, Rectangles, Finishing Triangles	Replacement Triangles
*WOF = Width of Fabric				
Assorted Medium and Darks (Cut from each of 4 fabrics)	Flying Geese	1 strip 7½" x WOF* from each fabric	(5) 7½" squares from each of the assorted fabrics, for a total of 20 squares	
Background	Rectangles	11 strips 6½" x WOF	(116) 3½" x 6½" rectangles (4) 3½" squares (Borders)	
	Flying Geese	8 strips 4" x WOF	(80) 4" squares	
	Border 3	8 strips 4" x WOF		
Tan	Replacement Triangles	9 strips 4" x WOF		98 Triangle Pairs
				98 Type 1 / 98 Type 2
	Border 2	7 strips 2" x WOF		
Light Gray	Replacement Triangles	9 strips 4" x WOF		
				40 Type 1 / 160 Type 2

Flying Geese

Refer to the Flying Geese Instructions on page 8.

Use the combinations below to make 3 ½" x 6 ½" Cut Size Flying Geese units.

- (80) 4" Background squares / (20) 7 ½" Assorted squares - make 80 FG units.

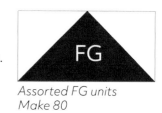

Assorted FG units
Make 80

Replacement Triangles

Refer to the Cutting Replacement Triangles for Type 1 and 2 on pages 18 and 19.

Use the 4" Cut Away Line to cut a total of

- (98) Tan Type 1 and 2 replacement triangle pairs*.

- (40) Light Gray Type 1 replacement triangle pairs*.

- (160) Light Gray Type 2 replacement triangle pairs*.

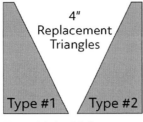

Tan - Make 98 Pairs

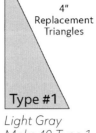

Light Gray
Make 40 Type 1

Light Gray
Make 160 Type 2

Note: Separate the Type 1 and 2 Replacement Triangles in two different stacks. I suggest using labeled Paper Plates to help keep yourself organized.

Popped Flying Geese Units

Refer to the Cut Away Corner Type 1 and Type 2 on pages 20 and 21. Press seams open.

First Side Pop - Type 1

1. Place a FG unit **Right Side Up**.

2. Using the **3" Cut Away Line,** trim along the edge of the FG base unit as shown.

Type 1 Cut Away

3. Referring to the FG diagram below, stitch a 3" Tan Type 1 Replacement Triangle to a FG base unit. Press seam open.

4. Place the FG unit **Wrong Side Up**. Trim by using the **3" Corner Trim Down Line** according to the instructions on page 21- step 7. Make a total of (80) FG units.

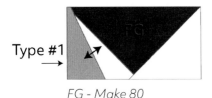

FG - Make 80

Second Side Pop -Type 2

1. Place a FG unit **Wrong Side Up**.

2. Using the **3" Cut Away Line,** trim along the edge of the FG unit as shown.

Type 2 Cut Away

3. Referring to the FG diagram, stitch a 3" Light Gray Type 2 Replacement Triangle to a FG unit. Press seam open.

4. Place the FG unit **Right Side Up**. Trim by using the **3" Corner Trim Down Line** according to the instructions on page 22- step 7. Make a total of (80) FG units.

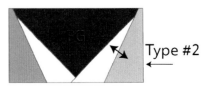

FG - Make 80

Popped Rectangle units

Refer to the Cut Away Corner Type 1 and Type 2 on pages 20 and 21. **Press seams open.**

First Side Pop - Type 1

1. Place a 3½" x 6½" Background rectangle **Right Side Up.**

2. Using the **3" Cut Away Line,** trim along the edge of the Background rectangle as shown to the right.

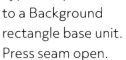

Type 1 Cut Away

3. Referring to the Unit A and B diagram below, stitch a 4" Type 1 Replacement Triangle to a Background rectangle base unit. Press seam open.

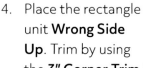

Type 1 Cut Away

4. Place the rectangle unit **Wrong Side Up**. Trim by using the **3" Corner Trim Down Line** according to the instructions on page 21- step 7.

5. Make a total of the following:

   - (40) Unit A using a 3½" x 6½" Background Rectangle / 4" Light Gray Type 1

   - (18) Unit B using a 3½" x 6½" Background Rectangle / 4" Tan Type 1

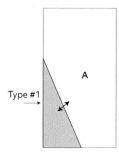

Unit A - Make 40

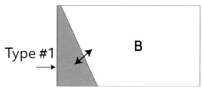

Unit B- Make 18

Second Side Pop -Type 2

1. Place a Unit A **Wrong Side Up**.

2. Using the **3" Cut Away Line,** trim the unit on the edge of the Unit A as shown.

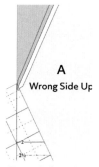

3. Referring to the Unit A diagram, stitch a 4" Type 2 Replacement Triangle to an Unit A. Press seam open.

Type 2 Cut Away

4. Place the Unit A **Right Side Up**. Trim by using the **3" Corner Trim Down Line** according to the instructions on page 22- step 7.

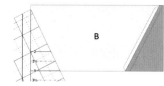

Type 2 Cut Away

5. Make a total of the following:

   - (40) Unit A / 4" Tan Type 2

   - (18) Unit B / 4" Light Gray Type 2

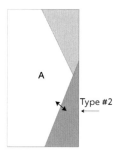

Unit A - Make 40

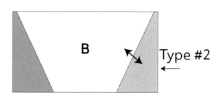

Unit B - Make 18

Popped Rectangle Units Cont...

Refer to the Cut Away Corner Type 2 on page 21. Press seams open.

First Side Pop - Type 2

1. Place a 3½" x 6½" Background rectangle base unit **Wrong Side Up**.

2. Using the **3" Cut Away Line**, trim the edge of the background rectangle as shown.

Type 1 Cut Away

3. Referring to the Unit C diagram, stitch a 4" Type 2 Replacement Triangle to a rectangle base unit. Press seam open.

4. Place the rectangle unit **Right Side Up**. Trim by using the **3" Corner Trim Down Line** according to the instructions on page 22- step 7.

5. Make a total of the following:

   - (40) Unit C, using a 3½" x 6½" background rectangle / 4" Tan Type 2

   - (18) Unit D, using a 3½" x 6½" background rectangle / 4" Light Gray Type 2

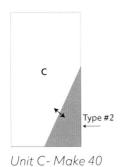

Unit C- Make 40

*Unit D
Make 18*

Second Side Pop -Type 2

1. Place a Unit A **Wrong Side Up**.

2. Using the **3" Cut Away Line**, trim the edge of Unit A as shown.

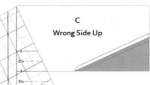

Type 2 Cut Away

3. Referring to the Unit A diagram, stitch a 4" Type 2 Replacement Triangle to an Unit A. Press seam open.

4. Place Unit A **Right Side Up**. Trim by using the **3" Corner Trim Down Line** according to the instructions on page 22- step 7.

5. Make a total of the following:

   - (40) Unit C / 4" Light Gray Type 2

   - (18) Unit D / 4" Tan Type 2

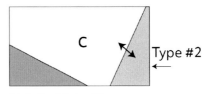

Unit C - Make 40

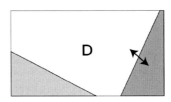

Unit D - Make 18

Popped Square Units

First Side Pop - Type 2

Refer to the Cut Away Corner Type 2 on page 21. Press seams open.

1. Place a 3½" Background square base unit **Wrong Side Up**.

2. Using the **3" Cut Away Line,** trim along the edge of the square.

3. Referring to the Unit E diagram, stitch a 3" Light Gray Type 2 Replacement Triangle to a Background square base unit. Press seam open.

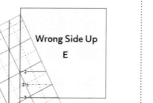

Type 2 Cut Away

4. Place the square **Right Side Up**. Trim by using the 3" **Corner Trim Down Line** according to the instructions on page 22- step 7. Make a total of (4) Unit E.

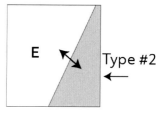

Unit E - Make 4

Combo Unit Assembly

Press seams as shown in diagrams.

1. Assemble (40) FG and (40) Unit A as shown. Make (40) 6 ½" Combo1 units.

2. Assemble (40) FG and (40) Unit B as shown. Make (40) 6 ½" Combo2 units.

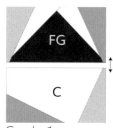

Combo1
Make 40

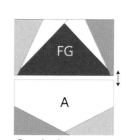

Combo2
Make 40

Block Assembly

1. Gather (2) Combo1 units / (2) Combo2 units.

2. Lay out the block according to the layout diagram shown.

3. Stitch the units into rows, pressing seams as shown in the diagram.

4. Stitch the rows together, pressing seams as shown in the diagram.

5. Repeat to make a total of (20) 12 ½" square block.

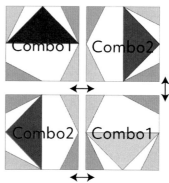

Block Layout - Make 20

Quilt Assembly

Quilt Center Assembly

1. Lay out the 12 ½" blocks as shown in the layout diagram.

2. Stitch the blocks into horizontal rows, and press as indicated in the diagram.

3. Stitch the rows together to create your quilt top, pressing as shown in the diagram.

Border 1 Pieced

4. Using the Pieced Border 1 instructions below, stitch the Side, Top and Bottom borders together.

5. Stitch the Pieced Border 1 according to the detailed instructions on page 33. Press according to quilt layout on page 77.

6. Using the "Join Border Pieces" detailed instructions on page 32, piece border 2 and 3 together.

Border 2 – Tan

Left and Right – Cut (4) 2" x WOF strips. Join together, cut (2) 2" x 66 ½"

Top and Bottom – Cut (3) 2" x WOF strips. Join together, cut (2) 2" x 57 ½"

Border 3 – Background

Left and Right – Cut (4) 4" x WOF strips. Join together, cut (2) 4" x 69 ½"

Top and Bottom – Cut (4) 4" x WOF strips. Join together, cut (2) 4" x 64 ½"

7. Stitch Borders 2 and 3 according to the detailed instructions on page 33. Press according to the quilt layout on page 77.

Border 1 Pieced

1. Gather (18) Unit D / (18) Unit C / (4) Unit E.

2. Stitch together (1) Unit D and (1) Unit C unit together to make 18, pressing each seam open to make (18) Border Pieces.

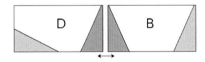

Border Pieces - Make 18

3. Stitch (5) Border Pieces side by side to make a side border strip as shown in the diagram below. Repeat to Make a total of (2) 3 ½" x 60 ½" side border strips.

Side Borders - Make 2

4. Stitch (4) Border Pieces side by side to make a top border strip as shown in the diagram below. Stitch (1) 3 ½" Unit E on each end of the top border strip, and repeat to make (2) 3 ½" x 54 ½" top and bottom border strips.

Top and Bottom Borders - Make 2

Finishing

Layer, quilt, and bind as desired.

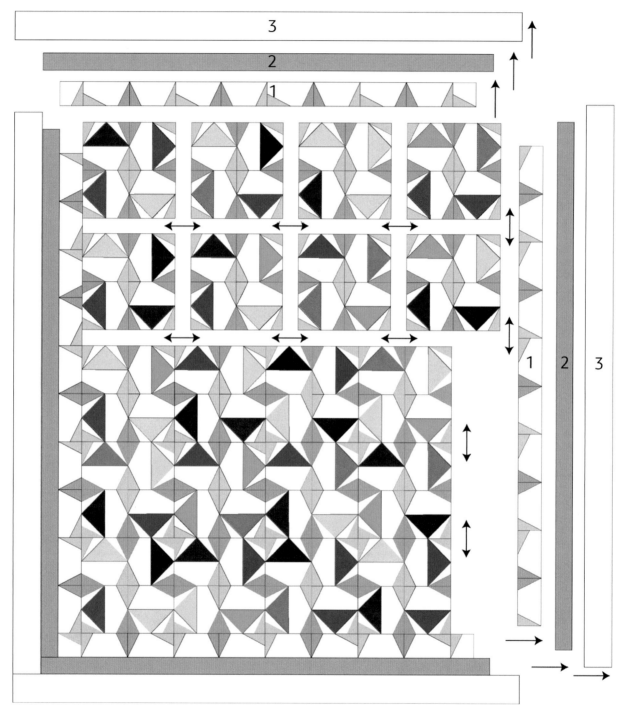

Scrappy Spinner Quilt Layout

Chapter 5 - Corner Pop III Projects

Blossom Sakura
60" x 60"
Page 81

Loose
48" x 48"
Page 91

Petal Spinner
60" x 60"
Page 98

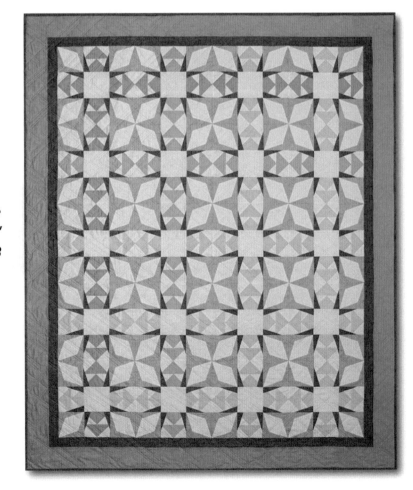

Mirrored Ombre
58" x 70"
Page 108

Project 5: Blossom Sakura
Finished Block: 12" x 12" · Finished Quilt: 60" x 60"

The term Sakura is the Japanese term for ornamental cherry blossoms. This quilt was designed while thinking of the annual Cherry Blossom Festival held every spring in the Washington DC area. It makes use of vibrant colors that will bring warmth and peace into your heart.

> Please read through the tool instructions of Corner Pop® III on pages 23-28 for detailed instructions. This will aid you in making the Popped units in this pattern.

Yardage

Based on 40" wide fabric, with an extra strip added for mistakes.

Cream – 3 yards

Lt. Pink – ½ yard

Pink – 1 ⅛ yards

Purple – 1 ⅛ yards

Black – ⅝ yards

Backing - 4 yards

Binding - ⅝ yard

Studio 180 Design Tools

Wing Clipper® I

Corner Pop® III

Quilter's Magic Wand

Unit Summary

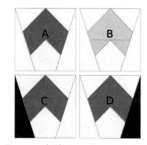

Popped Flying Geese Units
4 ½" Cut Size
(16) Unit A ~ (20) Unit B
(8) Unit C ~ (8) Unit D

Popped Corner Squares
4 ½" Cut Size
(8) Unit E

Popped Squares
4 ½" Cut Size
(8) Unit F ~ (8) Unit G

Squares
4 ½"
(28) Cream ~ (13) Purple

Cutting Chart

Color	Unit	Cut	Subcut	
			Squares, Rectangles, Finishing Triangles	Replacement Triangles
WOF = Width of Fabric				
Cream	Flying Geese	2 strips 5½" x WOF*	(13) 5½" squares	
	Replacement Triangles	4 strips 5" x WOF		44 Replacement Pairs
				44 Type 1 / 44 Type 2
	Squares	7 strips 4½" x WOF	(52) 4½" Squares. Divide into (3) stacks: (28) Corner Squares (8) Popped Corners Based Units (16) Popped Squares Based Units	
	Flying Geese	4 strips 3" x WOF	(52) 3" squares	
	Corner Setting Triangles	1 strip 9½" x WOF	(2) 9½" squares, cut diagonally once to yield (4) triangles.	
	Side Setting Triangles	1 strip 18½" x WOF	(2) 18½" squares, cut diagonally twice, to yield (8) triangles.	
Lt. Pink	Flying Geese	1 strip 5½" x WOF	(5) 5½" squares	
	Flying Geese	2 strips 3" x WOF	(20) 3" squares	
Pink	Flying Geese	2 strips 5½" x WOF	(8) 5½" squares	
	Flying Geese	3 strips 3" x WOF	(32) 3" squares	
	Border 1	6 strips 2" x WOF		
Purple	Center Squares	2 strips 4½" x WOF	(13) 4½" squares	
	Border 2	7 strips 3½" x WOF		
Black	Replacement Triangles	3 strips 5" x WOF.		32 Triangle Pairs
				32 Type 1 / 32 Type 2

Flying Geese

Refer to the Flying Geese Instructions on page 8.

Using the following fabric combinations make
2 ½" x 4 ½" cut size flying geese.

- (32) 3" Cream / (8) 5 ½" Pink squares - make (32) FG1 Units.

- (32) 3" Pink / (8) 5 ½" Cream squares - make (32) FG2 Units.

- (20) 3" Cream / (5) 5 ½" Lt. Pink squares - make (20) FG3 Units.

- (20) 3" Lt. Pink / (5) 5 ½" Cream squares – make (20) FG4 Units.

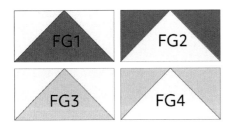

Flying Geese Units

Flying Geese Combination Assembly

Press seams as shown in diagrams.

1. Assemble (1) FG1 and (1) FG2 unit as shown to make (32) 4 ½" Combo1 units.

2. Assemble (1) FG3 and (1) FG4 unit as shown to make (20) 4 ½" Combo2 units.

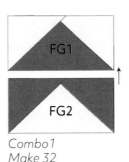
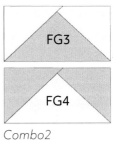

Combo1
Make 32

Combo2
Make 20

Replacement Triangles

Refer to the Cutting Replacement Triangles for Type 1 and 2 on pages 24 and 25.

Use the 5" Cut Away Line to cut a total of

- (44) Cream Type 1 and 2 replacement triangle pairs*.

- (32) Black Type 1 and 2 replacement triangle pairs*.

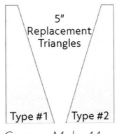

Cream - Make 44

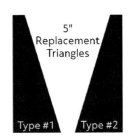

Black - Make 32

Note: Separate the Type 1 and 2 Replacement Triangles into two different stacks. I suggest using labeled Paper Plates to help keep yourself organized.

Popped Flying Geese

Refer to the Cut Away Corner Type 1 and 2 on pages 26 and 27. Press seams open.

First Side Pop - Type 1

1. Place a combo unit **Right side up**.

2. Using the **4" Cut Away Line,** trim along the edge of the combo base unit as shown

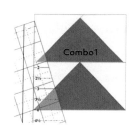

Type 1 Cut Away

3. Referring to the Combo 1 diagram, stitch a 5" Type 1 Replacement Triangle to the combo unit. Press seam open.

4. Place the Combo unit **Wrong Side Up**. Trim by using the **4" Corner Trim Down line** according to the instructions on page 27 - step 7.

5. Make a total of the following:

   - (24) Combo1 / Cream Type 1

   - (20) Combo2 / Cream Type 1

   - (8) Combo1 / Black Type 1

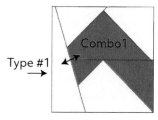

Combo1- Make 24

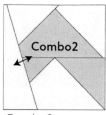

Combo2 Make 20

Combo3 Make 8

Second Side Pop - Type 2

1. Place a combo unit **Wrong Side up**.

2. Using the **4" Cut Away Line,** trim along the edge of the combo unit as shown

3. Referring to Unit A Diagram, stitch a 5" Type 2 Replacement Triangle to the combo unit. Press seam open.

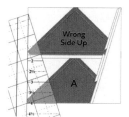

Type 2 Cut Away

4. Place the Combo unit **Right Side up**. Trim by using the **4" Corner Trim Down line** according to the instructions on page 28 - step 7.

5. Make a total of the following:

   - (16) Unit A using a Combo 1 / Cream Type 2

   - (20) Unit B using a Combo 1 / Cream Type 2

   - (8) Unit C using a Combo 1 / Cream Type 2

   - (8) Unit D using a Combo1 / Black Type 2

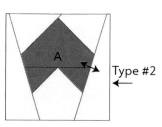

Unit A - Make 16

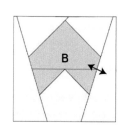

Unit B - Make 20

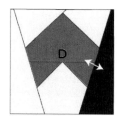

Unit D - Make 8

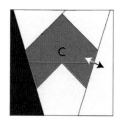

Unit C - Make 8

Popped Corner

Refer to the Cut Away Corner Type 1 and 2 on pages 26 and 27. Press seams open.

First Side Pop - Type 1

1. Place a 4 ½" Cream Pop Corner Square **Right Side Up.**

2. Using the **4" Cut Away Line,** trim along on the edge of the square.

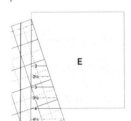

Type 1 Cut Away

3. Referring to the Unit E diagram, stitch a 5" Black Type 1 Replacement Triangle to the square. Press seam open.

4. Place the base square **Wrong Side Up**. Trim by using the **4" Corner Trim Down Line** according to the instructions on page 27 - step 7. Make a total of (8) Unit E.

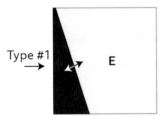

Unit E- Make 8

Second Side Pop - Type 2

1. Place a square **Wrong Side Up.**

2. Using the **4" Cut Away Line,** trim along the edge of the square.

Type 2 Cut Away

3. Referring to the Unit E diagram, stitch a 5" Black Type 2 Replacement Triangle to the square. Press seam open.

4. Place the square **Right Side Up.** Trim by using the **4" Corner Trim Down Line** according to the instructions on page 28 - step 7. Make a total of (8) Unit E.

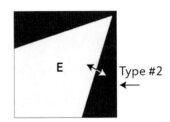

Unit E - Make 8

Popped Square

Refer to the Cut Away Corner Type 1 and 2 on pages 26 and 27. Press seams open.

First Side Pop - Type 1

1. Place a 4 ½" Cream square **Right Side Up**.

2. Using the **4" Cut Away Line,** trim along the edge of the square base unit.

Type 1 Cut Away

3. Referring to the Unit F diagram, stitch a 5" Black Type 1 Replacement Triangle to a Cream square base unit. Press seam open.

4. Place the square **Wrong Side Up**. Trim by using the **4" Corner Trim Down Line** according to the instructions on page 27 - step 7. Make a total of (8) Unit F units.

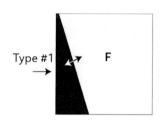

Unit F - Make 8

Second Side Pop

5. Turn Unit F **Right Side Up**, rotate according to the Type 1 Cut Away.

6. Using the **4" Cut Away line,** trim along on the edge of Unit F. Press seam open.

Type 1 Cut Away

7. Referring to the Unit F Second Side Diagram, stitch a 5" Black Type 1 Replacement Triangle to a Unit F. Press seam open.

8. Place the Unit F **Wrong Side Up**. Trim by using the **4" Corner Trim Down Line** according to the instructions on page 27 - step 7. Make a total of (8) Unit F.

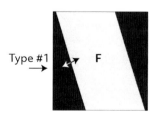

Unit F Second Side Make 8

First Side Pop - Type 2

1. Place a 4 ½" Cream Square **Wrong Side Up**.

2. Using the **4" Cut Away Line,** trim along the edge of the square base.

Type 2 Cut Away

3. Referring to the Unit G diagram, stitch a 5" Black Type 2 Replacement Triangle to a square base unit. Press seam open.

4. Place the square **Right Side Up.** Trim by using the **4" Corner Trim Down Line** according to the instructions on page 28 - step 7. Make a total of (8) Unit G.

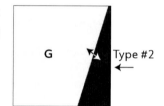

Unit G - Make 8

Second Side Pop

5. Turn Unit G **Wrong Side Up,** rotate according to the Type 2 Cut Away.

6. Using the **4" Cut Away line,** trim along the edge of Unit G.

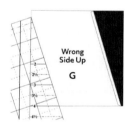

Type 2 Cut Away

7. Referring to the Unit G Second Side diagram, stitch a 5" Black Type 2 Replacement Triangle to a Unit G base unit. Press seam open.

8. Place the Unit G **Right Side Up.** Trim by using the **4" Corner Trim Down Line** according to the instructions on page 28 - step 7. Make a total of (8) Unit G.

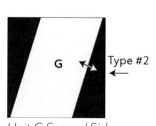

Unit G Second Side Make 8

Block 1 Assembly

Note: Press half of Block 1 one way, press the other half the other way according the diagrams.

1. Gather (2) Unit A / (1) Unit C / (1) Unit D / (1) Unit F unit / (1) Unit G / (1) 4 ½" Purple square / (2) 4 ½" Cream squares.

2. Lay out the block according to the layout diagram shown.

3. Stitch the units into rows, pressing seams as shown in the diagram. *(See the above note)*

4. Stitch the rows together, pressing seams as shown in the diagram. *(See the above note)*

5. Repeat to make a total of (8) 12 ½" square Block 1.

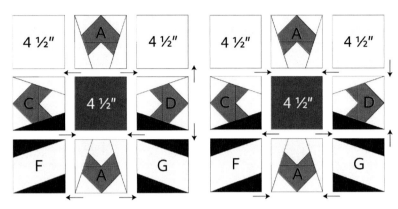

Block 1 Layout 1 - Make 4   *Block 1 Layout 2 - Make 4*

Block 2 Assembly

1. Gather (2) Unit E / (4) Unit B / (1) 4 ½" Purple square / (2) 4 ½" Cream squares.

2. Lay out the block according to the layout diagram shown.

3. Stitch the units into rows, pressing seams as shown in the diagram.

4. Stitch the rows together, pressing seams as shown in the diagram.

5. Repeat to make a total of (4) 12 ½" square Block 2.

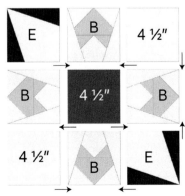

Block 2 Layout - Make 4

Block 3 Assembly

1. Gather (4) 4 ½" Cream squares / (4) Unit B units / (1) 4 ½" Purple square.

2. Lay out the block according to the layout diagram shown.

3. Stitch the units into rows, pressing seams as shown in the diagram.

4. Stitch the rows together, pressing seams as shown in the diagram.

5. Repeat to make a total of (1) 12 ½" square Block 3.

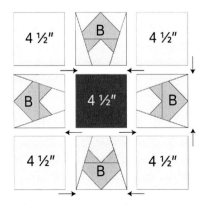

Block 3 Layout - Make 1

Quilt Assembly

1. Lay out the center blocks, side setting triangles, and corner setting triangles as shown in the layout diagram.

2. Stitch the blocks and Side Setting Triangles* into diagonal rows, pressing as shown in the diagram.

3. Stitch the rows together to create your quilt top, pressing seams open as shown in the diagram, being sure to add the top and bottom Corner Setting Triangles.

4. Trim all outside edges ¼".

   > ***Note:*** The side setting triangles are cut oversized! Carefully match the 90° corners of the setting triangles with the edges of the blocks. The opposite edge will be trimmed later.

5. Using the "Join Border Pieces" detailed instructions on page 32, piece the following together:

   Border 1 - Pink
   Left and Right – Cut (3) 2" x WOF strips. Join together, cut (2) 2" x 51 ½"
   Top and Bottom – Cut (3) 2" x WOF strips. Join together, cut (2) 2" x 54 ½"

   Border 2 - Purple
   Left and Right – Cut (3) 3 ½" x WOF strips. Join together, cut (2) 3 ½" x 54 ½"
   Top and Bottom – Cut (4) 3 ½" x WOF strips. Join together, cut (2) 3 ½" x 60 ½"

6. Stitch the Border 1 and 2 according to the detailed instructions on page 33. Press according to Quilt Layout on page 90.

Finishing

Layer, quilt, and bind as desired.

Side Setting
Triangle

Corner
Setting
Triangle

Block 2

Block 1

Block 1

Block 1

Block 2

Block 3

Block 2

Block 1

Block 1

Block 1

Block 2

Block 1

Blossom Sakura Quilt Layout

Project 6: Loose
Finished Block: 12" x 12" · Finished Quilt: 48" x 48"

Loose is a wall hanging designed to bring modern elegance into any space. The use of the neutral tones with arrowhead shapes provides a feel of motion like archers having just released their arrows.

> Please read through the tool instructions of Corner Pop III on pages 23-28 for detailed instructions. This will aid you in making the Popped units in this pattern.

Yardage

Based on 40" wide fabric, with an extra strip added for mistakes.

Background – 2 ⅜ yards

Light Green – 1 Fat Quarter

Green – 1 Fat Quarter

Light Blue – 1 Fat Quarter

Blue – 1 Fat Quarter

Backing - 3 ⅛ yards

Binding - ½ yard

Studio 180 Design Tools

Wing Clipper® I

Corner Pop® III

Quilter's Magic Wand

Unit Summary

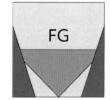

Popped Flying Geese Units
4 ½" Cut Size
(32) FG

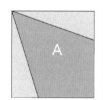

Popped Corner Squares
4 ½" Cut Size
(8) Unit A ~ (8) Unit B

Squares
4 ½"
(24) Background

Cutting Chart

Color	Unit	Cut	Squares, Rectangles, Finishing Triangles	Replacement Triangles	
WOF = Width of Fabric					
Background	Replacement Triangles	2 strips 5" x WOF*		16 Replacement Pairs	
				16 Type 1	16 Type 2
	Squares	3 strips 4½" x WOF	(24) 4½" squares		
	Rectangles	2 strips 4½" x WOF	(32) 2½" x 4½" rectangles		
	Flying Geese	3 strips 3" x WOF	(32) 3" squares		
	Layout Squares	3 strips 12½" x WOF	(8) 12½" squares		
Light Green	Flying Geese	3 strips 5½" x 20"	(8) 5½" squares		
Green	Replacement Triangles	4 strips 4" x 20"		32 Replacement Pairs	
				32 Type 1	32 Type 2
Light Blue	Popped Corner Base Square	2 strips 4½" x 20"	(8) 4½" squares		
Blue	Popped Corner Base Square	2 strips 4½" x 20"	(8) 4½" squares		

Flying Geese

Refer to the Flying Geese Instructions on page 8.

Use the fabric combinations below to make
2 ½" x 4 ½" cut size Flying Geese.

• (32) 3" Background / (8) 5 ½" Light Green
squares - make (32) FG Units.

FG - Make 32

Combo Unit Assembly

Press seams as shown in the diagram.

Assemble (32) FG units and (32) 2 ½" x 4 ½"
Background rectangles as shown. Make (32) FG units.

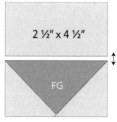

2 ½" x 4 ½"

FG

FG - Make 32

Replacement Triangles

Refer to the Cutting Replacement Triangles for Type 1 and 2 on pages 24 and 25.

1. Use the 5" Cut Away Line to cut a total of

   - (16) Background Type 1 and 2 replacement triangle pairs.

2. Use the 4" Cut Away Line to cut a total of

   - (32) Green Type 1 and 2 replacement triangles pairs.

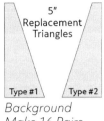
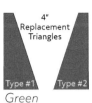

Background
Make 16 Pairs

Green
Make 32 Pairs

> **Note**: Separate the Type 1 and 2 Replacement Triangles in two different stacks. I suggest using labeled Paper Plates to help keep yourself organized.

Popped Flying Geese Units

Refer to the Cut Away Corner Type 1 and 2 on pages 26 and 27. Press seams open.

First Side Pop - Type 1

1. Place a FG base unit **Right Side Up**.

2. Using the **3" Cut Away Line**, trim along the edge of the unit as shown.

3. Referring to the FG Type 1 diagram, stitch a 4" Green Type 1 Replacement Triangle to the FG unit. Press seam open.

Type 1 Cut Away

4. Place the FG unit **Wrong Side Up**. Trim by using the **3" Corner Trim Down Line** according to the instructions on page 27- step 7. Make a total of (32) Popped FG units.

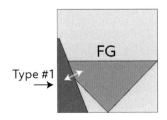

FG Type 1 - Make 32

Second Side Pop - Type 2

1. Place a FG unit **Wrong Side Up**.

2. Using the **3" Cut Away Line,** trim along the edges of the FG Unit as shown.

3. Referring to the FG Type 2 diagram, Stitch a 4" Green Type 2 Replacement Triangle to the FG unit. Press seam open.

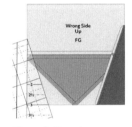

Type 2 Cut Away

4. Place the FG unit **Right Side Up**. Trim by using the **3" Corner Trim Down Line** according to the instructions on page 28 - step 7. Make a total of (32) Popped FG units.

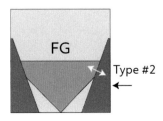

FG Type 2 - Make 32

Popped Corners (PC)

Refer to the Cut Away Corner Type 1 and 2 on pages 26 and 27. Press seams open.

First Side Pop - Type 1

1. Place a 4 ½" Base Square **Right Side Up**.

2. Using the **4" Cut Away Line,** trim along on the edge of the square as shown.

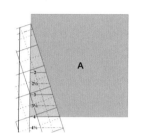

Type 1 Cut Away

3. Referring to the Unit A diagram, stitch a 5" Background Type 1 Replacement Triangle to the square. Press the seam open.

4. Place the square **Wrong Side Up**. Trim by using the **4" Corner Trim Down Line** according to the instructions on page 27 - step 7.

5. Make a total of the following:

   - (8) Unit A using a 4 ½" Light Blue Square / (8) 5" Background Type 1

   - (8) Unit B using 4 ½" Blue Square / (8) 5" Background Type 1

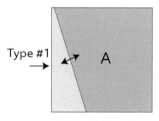

Unit A - Make 8   *Unit B- Make 8*

Second Side Pop - Type 2

1. Place a square **Wrong Side Up**.

2. Using the **4" Cut Away Line,** trim along the edge of the square as shown.

3. Referring to the Unit A diagram, stitch a 5" Background Type 2 Replacement Triangle to a square unit. Press seams open.

Type 2 Cut Away

4. Place the square **Right Side Up**. Trim by using the **4" Corner Trim Down Line** according to the instructions on page 28 - step 7.

5. Make a total of the following:

   - (8) Unit A / (8) 5" Background Type 2

   - (8) Unit B / (8) 5" Background Type 2

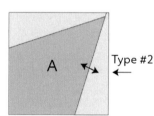

Unit A - Make 8   *Unit B - Make 8*

Block Assembly

1. Gather (4) FG units / (1) Unit A / (1) Unit B / (3) 4 ½" Background squares.

2. Lay out the block according to the layout diagram shown.

3. Stitch the units into rows, pressing seams as shown in the diagram.

4. Stitch the rows together, pressing seams as shown in the diagram.

5. Repeat to make a total of (8) 12 ½" square Block.

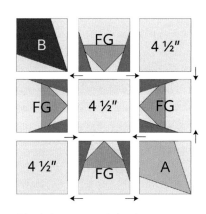

Block Layout - Make 8

Quilt Assembly

1. Lay out the 12 ½" Blocks as shown in the layout diagram. Pay attention to the block placement.

2. Stitch the blocks into horizontal rows, and press as indicated in the diagram.

3. Stitch the rows together to create your quilt top, pressing as shown in the diagram on page 97.

Finishing

Layer, quilt, and bind as desired.

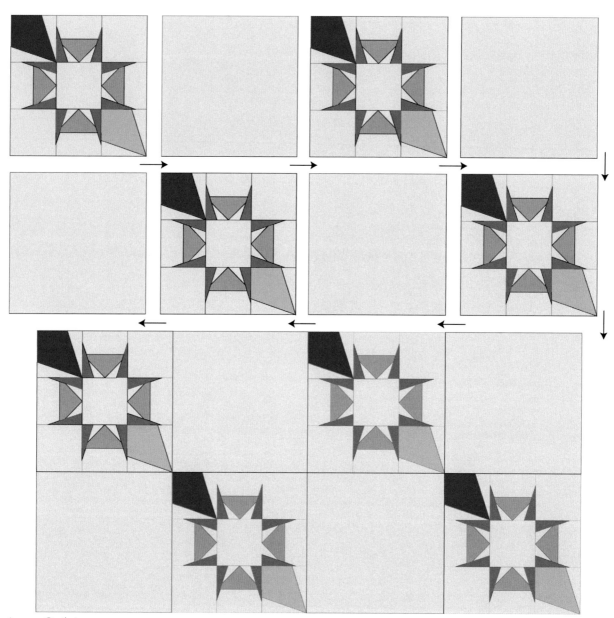

Loose Quilt Layout

Project 7: Petal Spinner

Finished Block: 12" x 12" · Finished Quilt: 60" x 60"

Feel the twirling and spinning as the blowing wind provides motion to the flower petals in this wall hanging quilt pattern. The spinning comes from the use of different fan shapes inside of fan shapes and adds interest to the overall design. This design utilizes a balance of both warm and cool colors, but use your imagination to add that personal appeal to the design.

> Please read through the tool instructions of Corner Pop III on pages 23-28 for detailed instructions. This will aid you in making the Popped units in this pattern.

Yardage

Based on 40" wide fabric, with an extra strip added for mistakes.

Background – 2 ½ yards
Accent1 (White Floral) – 1 yard
Accent2 (Green Floral) – ⅓ yard
Accent3 (Pink Floral) - ⅞ yard
Orange – Fat Quarter
Yellow – Fat Quarter
Light Red – ¾ yard

Light Blue – ⅜ yard
Medium Red - Fat Quarter
Medium Blue - Fat Quarter
Dark Red – ⅝ yard
Dark Blue – ⅝ yard
Backing - 3 ⅞ yards
Binding - ⅝ yard

Studio 180 Design Tools

Wing Clipper® I
Corner Pop® III
Quilter's Magic Wand

Unit Summary

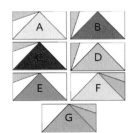

Popped Flying Geese Units
3 ½" x 6 ½" Cut Size
(16) Unit A ~ (8) Unit B
(8) Unit C ~ (8) Unit D
(8) Unit E ~ (8) Unit F
(8) Unit G

Popped Pickets Units
3 ½" x 6 ½" Cut Size
(16) Unit H ~ (16) Unit I

Popped Rectangles Units
3 ½" x 6 ½" Cut Size
(16) Unit J ~ (16) Unit K

Cutting Chart

Color	Unit	Cut	Squares, Rectangles, Finishing Triangles	Replacement Triangles	
		WOF = Width of Fabric			
Background	Picket	4 strips 6¾" x WOF*	(32) 3¾" x 6¾" rectangles		
	Rectangles	3 strips 6½" x WOF	(32) 3½" x 6½" rectangles		
	Replacement Triangles	1 strip 4" x WOF		Type 2 Only	
					32 Type 2
	Flying Geese	5 strips 4" x WOF	(48) 4" squares		
	Flying Geese	2 strips 3¾" x WOF	(16) 3¾" squares		
Accent1 (White Floral)	Replacement Triangles	1 strip 4" x WOF		Type 2 Only	
					16 Type 2
	Flying Geese	1 strip 7½" x WOF	(4) 7½" squares		
Accent2 (Green Floral)	Replacement Triangles	2 strips 4" x WOF		32 Replacement Pairs	
				32 Type 1	32 Type 2
	Border 2	6 strips 2" x WOF			
Orange	Squares	4 strips 3¾" x 20"	(16) 3¾" squares		
Yellow	Replacement Triangles	1 strip 4" x WOF		Type 2 Only	
					16 Type 2
Light Red	Flying Geese	1 strip 6¾" x WOF	(8) 3¾" x 6¾" rectangles		
	Border 1	6 strips 2" x WOF			
Light Blue	Flying Geese	1 strip 6¾" x WOF	(8) 3¾" x 6¾" rectangles		
Medium Red	Flying Geese	1 strip 7½" x 20"	(2) 7½" squares		
Medium Blue	Flying Geese	1 strip 7½" x 20"	(2) 7½" squares		
Dark Red	Flying Geese	1 strip 7½" x WOF	(2) 7½" squares		
	Popped Pickets	2 strips 3¾" x WOF	(16) 3¾" squares		
Dark Blue	Flying Geese	1 strip 7½" x WOF	(2) 7½" squares		
	Popped Pickets	2 strips 3¾" x WOF	(16) 3¾" squares		
Accent3	Border 3	7 strips 3½" x WOF			

Flying Geese

Refer to the Flying Geese Instructions on page 8.

Use the fabric combinations below to make 3 ½" x 6 ½" Cut Size Flying Geese units.

- (16) 4" Background squares / (4) 7 ½" Accent1 squares - make (16) FG1 Units.

- (8) 4" Background squares / (2) 7 ½" Medium Red squares - make (8) FG2 Units.

- (8) 4" Background squares / (2) 7 ½" Medium Blue squares - make (8) FG3 Units.

- (8) 4" Background squares / (2) 7 ½" Dark Red squares - make (8) FG4 Units.

- (8) 4" Background squares / (2) 7 ½" Dark Blue squares - make (8) FG5 Units.

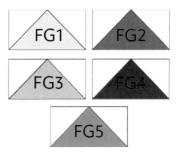

Flying Geese Units

Stitch and Flip Flying Geese

Refer to the Stitch and Flip Instructions on page 10.

We will make these Flying Geese so that the Background wing is on the left and Orange wing is on the right every time.

Use the following combinations to make 3 ½" x 6 ½" Cut Size Flying Geese units using the Stitch and Flip Method.

- (8) 3 ¾" Background squares / (8) 3 ¾" x 6 ¾" Light Red Rectangles / (8) 3 ¾" Orange squares - make (8) FG6 Units.

- (8) 3 ¾" Background squares / (8) 3 ¾" x 6 ¾" Light Blue Rectangles / (8) 3 ¾" Orange squares - make (8) FG7 Units.

Stitch and Flip units
Make (8) FG6 and (8) FG7

Replacement Triangles

Refer to the Cutting Replacement Triangles for Type 1 and 2 on pages 24 and 25.

Use the 4" Cut Away Line to cut a total of:

- (32) Accent2 Type 1 and 2 Replacement Triangles pairs*.

- (32) Background Type 2 Replacement Triangles*.

> ***Note:*** Separate the Type 1 and 2 Replacement Triangles in two different stacks. I suggest using labeled Paper Plates to help keep yourself organized.

- (16) Accent1 Type 2 Replacement Triangles*.

- (16) Yellow Type 2 Replacement Triangles*.

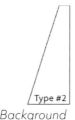

Accent2
Make 32 Pairs

Background
Make 32 Type 2

Accent1
Make 16 Type 2

Yellow
Make 16 Type 2

Popped Flying Geese Units

Refer to the Cut Away Corner Type 1 and 2 on pages 26 and 27. Press seams open.

First Side Pop - Type 1

1. Place a FG unit **Right Side Up**.

2. Using the **3" Cut Away Line,** trim along the edge of FG unit as shown.

3. Referring to the Unit A diagram below, stitch a 4" Accent2 Type 1 Replacement Triangle to a FG base unit. Press seam open.

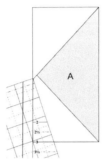

Type 1 Cut Away

4. Place the FG unit **Wrong Side Up**. Trim by using the **3" Corner Trim Down Line** according to the instructions on page 27 - step 7.

5. Make a total of the following:

   - (16) Unit A using a FG1 / 4" Accent2 Type 1

   - (8) Unit C using a FG5 / 4" Accent2 Type 1

   - (8) Unit E using a FG4 / 4" Accent2 Type 1

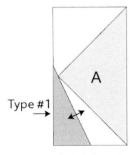

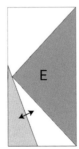

Unit A- Make 16

Unit C Make 8

Unit E Make 8

First Side Pop - Type 2

1. Place a FG unit **Wrong Side Up**.

2. Using the **3" Cut Away Line,** trim along the edge of the FG unit as shown.

Type 2 Cut Away

3. Referring to the Unit B diagram below, stitch a 4" Type 2 Replacement Triangle to a FG unit. Press seam open.

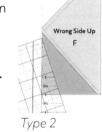

4. Place the FG unit **Right Side Up**. Trim by using the **3" Corner Trim Down Line** according to the instructions on page 28 - step 7.

Type 2 Cut Away

5. Make a total of the following:

   - (8) Unit B, using a FG2 / 4" Accent2 Type 2

   - (8) Unit D, using a FG3 / 4" Accent2 Type 2

   - (8) Unit F, using a FG7 / 4" Yellow Type 2

   - (8) Unit G, using a FG6 / 4" Yellow Type 2

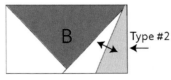
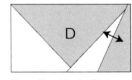

Unit B - Make 8

Unit D - Make 8

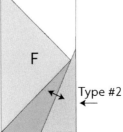

Unit F - Make 8

Unit G Make 8

Pickets

Refer to the Picket Instructions on page 13.

Use the following combinations to make 3 ½" x 6 ½" Cut Size Picket units.

- (16) 3 ¾" Dark Red squares / (16) 3 ¾" x 6 ¾" Background Rectangles - make (16) Picket1

- (16) 3 ¾" Dark Blue squares / (16) 3 ¾" x 6 ¾" Background Rectangles - make (16) Picket2

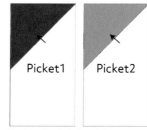

Picket1 - Make 16
Picket2 - Make 16

Popped Pickets Units

Refer to the Cut Away Corner Type 2 on page 27. Press seams open.

First Side Pop - Type 2

1. Place a Picket unit **Wrong Side Up**.

2. Using the **3" Cut Away Line,** trim along the edge of the unit as shown.

Type 2 Cut Away

3. Referring to the Unit H diagram, stitch a 4" Background Type 2 Replacement Triangle to a unit. Press seam open.

4. Place the Picket unit **Right Side Up**. Trim by using the **3" Corner Trim Down Line** according to the instructions on page 28 - step 7.

5. Make a total of the following:

- (16) Unit H using a Picket1 / 4" Background Type 2

- (16) Unit I using a Picket2 / 4" Background Type 2

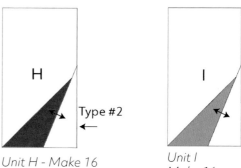

Unit H - Make 16

Unit I Make 16

Popped Rectangle Units

Refer to the Cut Away Corner Type 2 on page 27. Press seams open.

First Side Pop - Type 2

1. Place a Background Rectangle **Wrong Side Up**.

2. Using the **3" Cut Away Line,** trim along the edges of the rectangle as shown.

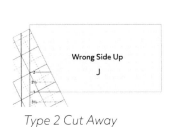

Type 2 Cut Away

Type 2 Cut Away

3. Referring to the Unit J and K diagrams below, stitch a 4" Type 2 Replacement Triangle to a Background rectangle. Press seam open.

4. Place the rectangle **Right Side Up**. Trim by using the **3" Corner Trim Down Line** according to the instructions on page 28 - step 7.

5. Make a total of the following:

   - (16) Unit J / 4" Accent2 Type 2

   - (16) Unit K / 4" Accent1 Type 2

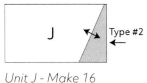

Unit J - Make 16

Unit K - Make 16

Combination Units

Press seams according to diagrams.

Assemble the following combination units as shown.

- (8) Combo1, using a Unit H / Unit A

- (8) Combo2, using a Unit B / Unit G

- (8) Combo3, using a Unit C / Unit K

- (8) Combo4, using a Unit H / Unit J

- (8) Combo5, using a Unit I / Unit A

- (8) Combo6, using a Unit D / Unit F

- (8) Combo7, using a Unit E / Unit K

- (8) Combo8, using a Unit I / Unit J

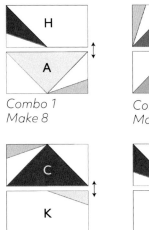

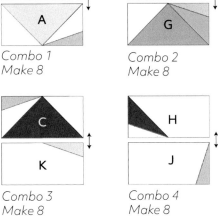

Combo 1
Make 8

Combo 2
Make 8

Combo 3
Make 8

Combo 4
Make 8

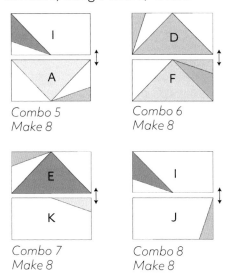

Combo 5
Make 8

Combo 6
Make 8

Combo 7
Make 8

Combo 8
Make 8

Block 1 Assembly

1. Gather (1) Combo 1 / (1) Combo 2 / (1) Combo 3 / (1) Combo 4 units.

2. Lay out the block according to the layout diagram shown.

3. Stitch the units into rows, pressing seams as shown in the diagram.

4. Stitch the rows together, pressing seams as shown in the diagram.

5. Repeat to make a total of (8) 12 ½" square Block 1.

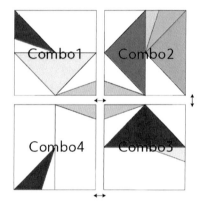

Block1 Layout - Make 8

6. Stitch (4) Block 1's together, rotating the blocks so the blocks spin, as shown in the diagram. Repeating to make (2) 24 ½" square Red Blocks.

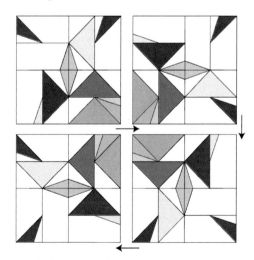

Red Blocks - Make 2

Block 2 Assembly

1. Gather (1) Combo 5 / (1) Combo 6 / (1) Combo 7 / (1) Combo 8 units.

2. Lay out the block according to the layout diagram shown.

3. Stitch the units into rows, pressing seams as shown in the diagram.

4. Stitch the rows together, pressing seams as shown in the diagram.

5. Repeat to make a total of (8) 12 ½" square Block 2.

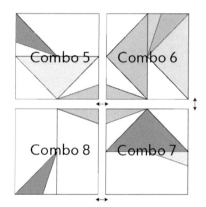

Block 2 Layout - Make 8

6. Stitch (4) Block 2's together, rotating the blocks so the blocks spin, as shown in the diagram. Repeating to make (2) 24 ½" square Blue Blocks.

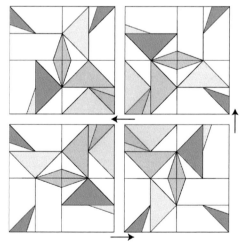

Blue Blocks - Make 2

Quilt Assembly

1. Lay out the 24 ½" Red Blocks and Blue Blocks as shown in the layout diagram.

2. Stitch the blocks into horizontal rows, and press as indicated in the diagram.

3. Stitch the rows together to create your quilt top, pressing as shown in the diagram.

4. Trim all outside edges ¼".

5. Using the "Join Border Pieces" detailed instructions on page 32, piece the following together:

   Border 1 - Lt. Red
   Left and Right – Cut (3) 2" x WOF strips. Join together, cut (2) 2" x 48 ½"
   Top and Bottom – Cut (3) 2" x WOF strips. Join together, cut (2) 2" x 51 ½"

   Border 2 – Accent2
   Left and Right – Cut (3) 2" x WOF strips. Join together, cut (2) 2" x 51 ½"
   Top and Bottom – Cut (3) 2" x WOF strips. Join together, cut (2) 2" x 54 ½"

   Border 3 – Accent3
   Left and Right – Cut (3) 3 ½" x WOF strips. Join together, cut (2) 3 ½" x 54 ½"
   Top and Bottom – Cut (4) 3 ½" x WOF strips. Join together, cut (2) 3 ½" x 60 ½"

6. Stitch Border 1, 2 and 3 according to the detailed instructions on page 33. Press according to the quilt layout on page 107.

Finishing

Layer, quilt, and bind as desired.

Petal Spinner Quilt Layout

Project 8: Mirrored Ombre

Finished Block: 12" x 12" · Finished Quilt: 58" x 70"

Ombre is the shading of color from light to dark, which you can see in the gentle flowing of the cool tones in this graceful lap quilt. If you are feeling more adventurous, you could choose fabrics with a greater value difference to create a more dramatic flair. Let your imagination be your guide.

> Please read through the tool instructions of Corner Pop III on pages 23-28 for detailed instructions. This will aid you in making the Popped units in this pattern.

Yardage

Based on 40" wide fabric, with an extra strip added for mistakes.

Assorted Fabrics (5 Fabric Values)
Dark - 1 ⅜ yards
Medium-Dark - 1 Fat Quarter
Medium - 1 Fat Quarter
Light1- 1 Fat Quarter
Light2- 1 Fat Quarter

Background – 3 yards
Gray – 2 yards
Dark Gray – 1 ½ yards
Backing - 3 ¾ yards
Binding - ⅝ yard

Studio 180 Design Tools

Wing Clipper® I
Corner Pop® III
Quilter's Magic Wand

Unit Summary

Popped Flying Geese Units
4 ½" Cut Size
(18) FG1 ~ (18) FG2
(18) FG3 ~ (18) FG4
(8) FG5

Double Popped
Corners
4 ½" Cut Size
(80) Unit A

Squares
4 ½"
(20) Background

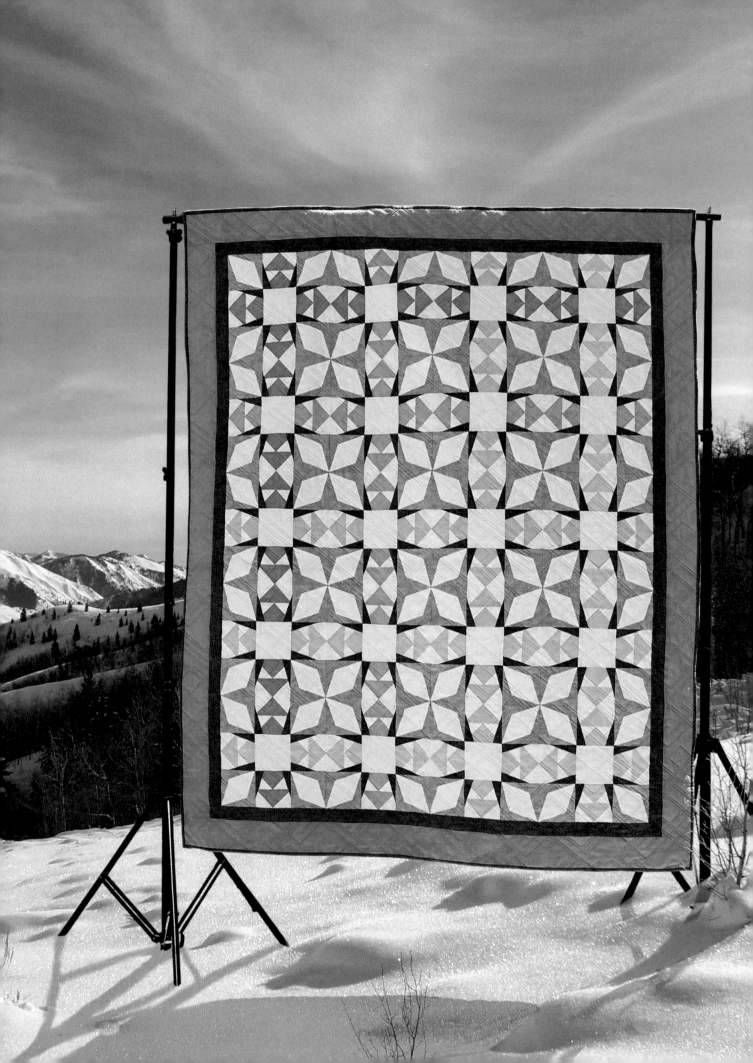

Cutting Chart

Color	Unit	Cut	Subcut	
			Squares, Rectangles, Finishing Triangles	Replacement Triangles
WOF = Width of Fabric				
Background	Popped Corner Base Unit	10 strips 4½" x WOF*	(80) 4½" squares	
	Center Squares	3 strips 4½" x WOF	(20) 4½" squares	
	Flying Geese	13 strips 3" x WOF	(160) 3" squares	
Gray	Replacement Triangles	13 strips 5" x WOF		160 Replacement Pairs
				160 Type 1 · 160 Type 2
Dark Gray	Replacement Triangles	5 strips 4" x WOF		80 Replacement Pairs
				80 Type 1 · 80 Type 2
	Border 1	7 strips 4" x WOF		
Dark	Flying Geese	2 strips 5½" x WOF	(9) 5½" squares	
	Border 2	8 strips 2" x WOF		
Medium-Dark	Flying Geese	3 strips 5½" x 20"	(9) 5½" squares	
Medium	Flying Geese	3 strips 5½" x 20"	(9) 5½" squares	
Light 1	Flying Geese	3 strips 5½" x 20"	(9) 5½" squares	
Light 2	Flying Geese	1 strip 5½" x 20"	(4) 5½" squares	

Flying Geese

Refer to the Flying Geese Instructions on page 8.

Use the fabric combinations below to make 2 ½" x 4 ½" cut size flying geese units.

- (36) 3" Background squares / (9) 5 ½" Dark squares - make (36) FG1

- (36) 3" Background squares / (9) 5 ½" Medium-Dark squares - make (36) FG2

- (36) 3" Background squares / (9) 5 ½" Medium squares - make (36) FG3

- (36) 3" Background squares / (9) 5 ½" Light1 squares - make (36) FG4

- (16) 3" Background squares / (4) 5 ½" Light2 squares - make (16) FG5

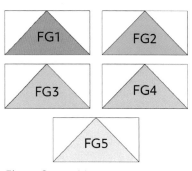

Flying Geese Units

Flying Geese Combination

Press seams according to the diagram.

Assemble the following Flying Geese (FG) units as shown.

- (36) FG1 together to make (18) FG1 units.
- (36) FG2 together to make (18) FG2 units.
- (36) FG3 together to make (18) FG3 units.

- (36) FG4 together to make (18) FG4 units.
- (16) FG5 together to make (8) FG5 units.

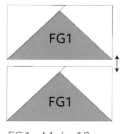

FG1 - Make 18

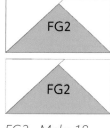

FG2 - Make 18

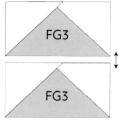

FG3 - Make 18

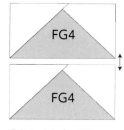

FG4 - Make 18

FG5 - Make 8

Replacement Triangles

Refer to the Cutting Replacement Triangles for Type 1 and 2 on pages 24 and 25.

1. Use the 4" Cut Away Line for the 4" strips to cut a total of

   - (80) 4" Dark Gray Type 1 and 2 replacement triangle pairs*.

2. Use the 5" Cut Away for the 5" strips to cut a total of

   - (160) 5" Gray Type 1 and 2 replacement triangle pairs*.

Dark Gray
Make 80 Pairs

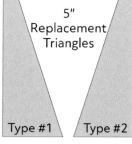

Gray - Make 160 Pairs

> ***Note:*** Separate the Type 1 and 2 Replacement Triangles in two different stacks. I suggest using labeled Paper Plates to help keep yourself organized.

Popped FG Units

Refer to the Cut Away Corner Type 1 and Type 2 on pages 26 and 27. Press seams open.

First Side Pop - Type 1

1. Place a FG unit **Right Side Up**.

2. Using the **3" Cut Away Line**, trim along the edge of the FG base unit as shown.

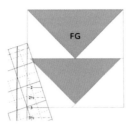

Type 1 Cut Away

3. Referring to the FG Type 1 diagram below, stitch a 4" Dark Gray Type 1 Replacement Triangle to a FG base unit. Press seam open.

4. Place the FG unit **Wrong Side Up**. Trim by using the **3" Corner Trim Down Line** according to the instructions on page 27 - step 7. Make a total of (80) using all FG units.

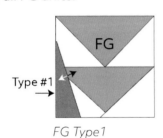

FG Type1

Second Side Pop - Type 2

1. Place a FG unit **Wrong Side Up**.

2. Using the **3" Cut Away Line**, trim along the edge of the FG units as shown.

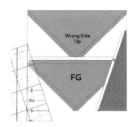

Type 1 Cut Away

3. Referring to the FG Type 2 Diagram below, stitch a 4" Dark Gray Type 2 Replacement Triangle to a FG unit. Press seam open.

4. Place the FG unit **Right Side Up**. Trim by using the **3" Corner Trim Down Line** according to the instructions on page 28 - step 7. Make a total of (80) FG units.

5. Sort the FG units by color.

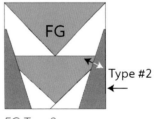

FG Type2

Double Popped Corners

Refer to the Cut Away Corner Type 1 and Type 2 on pages 26 and 27. Press seams open.

Corner 1 - First Side Pop - Type 1

1. Place a 4 ½" Background base square **Right Side Up**.

2. Using the **4" Cut Away Line**, trim along on the edge of the Background base square as shown.

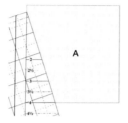

Type 1 Cut Away

3. Referring to the Corner 1 Type 1 diagram, stitch a 5" Gray Type 1 Replacement Triangle to a Background square base unit. Press seam open.

4. Place the unit **Right Side Up**. Trim by using the **4" Corner Trim Down Line** according to the instructions on page 27 - step 7. Make a total of (80) Unit A.

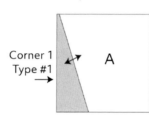

Corner 1 Type 1
Make 80

Second Side Pop - Type 2

5. Place a Unit A **Wrong Side Up**.

6. Using the **4" Cut Away Line**, trim along the edge of Unit A as shown.

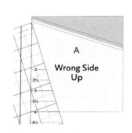

Type 2 Cut Away

7. Referring to the Unit A Type 2 diagram, stitch a 5" Gray Type 2 Replacement Triangle to a Unit A. Press seam open.

8. Place Unit A **Right Side Up**. Trim by using the **4" Corner Trim Down Line** according to the instructions on page 28 - step 7. Make a total of (80) Unit A.

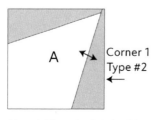

Unit A Type 2 - Make 80

Corner 2 - First Side Pop - Type 1

1. Place a Unit A **Right Side Up**.

2. Using the **4" Cut Away Line**, trim along on the edge of Unit A as shown.

3. Referring to the Corner 2 Type 1 diagram, stitch a 5" Gray Type 1 Replacement Triangle to a Unit A. Press seam open.

Type 1 Cut Away

4. Place a Unit A **Wrong Side Up** on your mat. Trim by using the **4" Corner Trim Down Lin** according to the instructions on page 27 - step 7. Make a total of (80) Unit A.

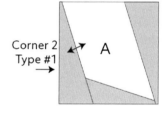

Corner 2 Type1 - Make 80

Second Side Pop - Type 2

5. Place a Unit A **Wrong Side Up**.

6. Using the **4" Cut Away Line**, trim along the edges of the of the Unit A as shown.

7. Referring to the Unit A Type 2 diagram, stitch a 5" Gray Type 2 Replacement Triangle to an Unit A. Press seams open.

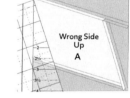

Type 2 Cut Away

8. Place Unit A **Right Side Up**. Trim by using the **4" Corner Trim Down Line** according to the instructions on page 28 - step 7. Make a total of (80) Unit A.

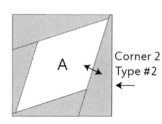

Unit A Type 2 - Make 80

Block Assembly

1. Lay out the units according to the block layout diagrams shown.

2. Stitch the units into rows, pressing seams as shown in the diagram.

3. Stitch the rows together, pressing seams as shown in the diagram .

4. Make the total of the following 12 ½" Blocks:

- (1) Block 1 using (4) FG1 / (4) Unit A /
  (1) 4 ½" Background center square.

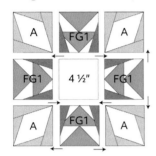

Block1 Layout - Make 1

- (2) Block 2 using (2) FG1 / (2) FG2 / (4) Unit A /
  (1) 4 ½" Background center square.

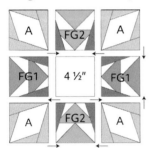

Block 2 - Make 2

- (2) Block 3 using (2) FG1 / (2) FG3 / (4) Unit A /
  (1) 4 ½" Background center square.

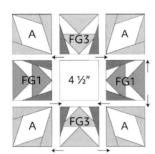

Block 3 - Make 2

- (2) Block 4 using (2) FG1 / (2) FG4/ (4) Unit A /
  (1) 4 ½" Background center square.

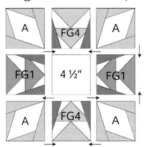

Block 4 - Make 2

- (1) Block 5 using (2) FG1 / (2) FG5 / (4) Unit A /
  (1) 4 ½" Background center square.

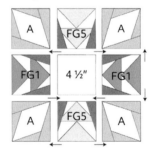

Block 5 - Make 1

- (1) Block 6 using (4) FG2 / (4) Unit A /
  (1) 4 ½" Background center square.

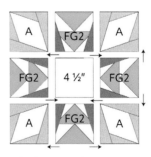

Block 6 - Make 1

- (2) Block 7 using (2) FG2 / (2) FG3 / (4) Unit A / (1) 4 ½" Background center square.

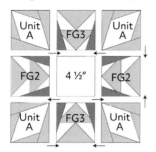

Block 7 - Make 2

- (2) Block 8 using (2) FG2 / (2) FG4 / (4) Unit A / (1) 4 ½" Background center square.

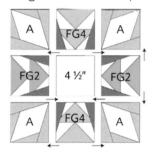

Block 8 - Make 2

- (1) Block 9 using (2) FG2 / (2) FG5 / (4) Unit A / (1) 4 ½" Background center square.

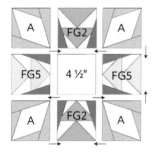

Block 9 - Make 1

- (1) Block 10 using (4) FG3 / (4) Unit A / (1) 4 ½" Background center square.

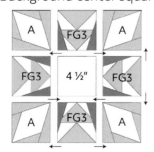

Block 10 - Make 1

- (2) Block 11 using (2) FG3 / (2) FG4 / (4) Unit A / (1) 4 ½" Background center square.

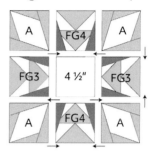

Block 11 - Make 2

- (1) Block 12 using (2) FG3 / (2) FG5 / (4) Unit A / (1) 4 ½" Background center square.

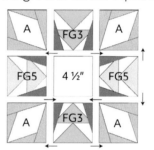

Block 12 - Make 1

- (1) Block 13 using (4) FG4 / (4) Unit A / (1) 4 ½" Background center square.

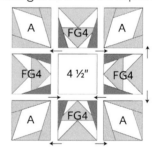

Block 13 - Make 1

- (1) Block 14 using (2) FG4 / (2) FG5 / (4) Unit A / (1) 4 ½" Background center square.

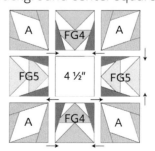

Block 14 - Make 1

Quilt Assembly

1. Lay out the 12 ½" Blocks as shown in the layout diagram. Pay attention to the block placement.

2. Stitch the blocks into horizontal rows, and press as indicated in the diagram.

3. Stitch the rows together to create your quilt top, pressing as shown in the diagram.

4. Trim all outside edges ¼".

5. Using the "Join Border Pieces" detailed instructions on page 32, piece the following together:

   Border 1 – Dark Gray
   Left and Right – Cut (4) 2" x WOF strips. Join together, cut (2) 2" x 60 ½"
   Top and Bottom – Cut (3) 2" x WOF strips. Join together, cut (2) 2" x 51 ½"

   Border 2 - Dark Fabric
   Left and Right – Cut (4) 4" x WOF strips. Join together, cut (2) 4" x 63 ½"
   Top and Bottom – Cut (4) 4" x WOF strips. Join together, cut (2) 4" x 58 ½"

6. Stitch Border 1 and 2 according to the detailed instructions on page 33. Pressing according to the quilt layout on page 117.

Finishing

1. Layer, quilt, and bind as desired

Mirrord Ombre Quilt Layout

Appendix: Fabric and Quilting Information

Project 1: Asterisk Star

Fabric: Timeless Treasures, Belle Filagree, Mix Basics; Dear Stella Dash Flow Basic

Quilt Design: Paisley Garden Grand by Bethenne Nemish , Urban Elementz

Project 2: Echo Star

Fabric: Timeless Treasures Mixed Basics Collection

Quilting Design: Friction by Karlee Porter, Karlee Porter Designs

Project 3: Nautical Sails

Fabric: Island Batik Foundation Collection

Quilting Design: Wave Pano 006 by Kimberly Diamond, Sweet Dreams Quilt Studio

Project 4: Scrappy Spinner

Fabric: Moda Grunge Fabrics, and various scraps.

Quilting Design: Modern MO Pano 001 by Kimberly Diamond, Sweet Dreams Quilt Studio

Project 5: Blossom Sakura

Fabric: Timeless Treasures Solid-ish Collection by Kimberly Einmo

Quilting Design: Asian Beauty by Nancy Haacke, Wasatch Quilting

Project 6: Loose

Fabric: KimberBell Basics, Maywood Studios; Hash Dot, Micheal Miller Basics; Solid-ish by Kimberly Einmo, Timeless Treasures

Quilting Design: Retro Lines by Kristin Hoftyzer, Urban Elementz

Project 7: Petal Spinner

Fabric: Isabella by Lily ashburn, Micheal Miller Fabrics

Quilting Design: Poppy Feathers by Jessica Schick, Urban Elementz

Project 8: Mirrored Ombre

Fabric: Timeless Treasures Mixed Basics Collection

Quilting Design: Pickup Sticks by Anne Bright, Anne Bright Studios

Quilting Done by Januari Rhodes, The Quilted Ginger, www.thequiltedginger.com; https://www.facebook.com/TheQuiltedGinger/

About the Author

Tina Dillard first began quilting back in 1995 with a quilt sampler class and fell in love with all aspects of quilting, even hand quilting. With a desire to launch a quilting business, she quit her government job in 2012, and she opened a longarm service and online fabric store. As a professional quilter, Tina was also learning the art of designing quilts in Electric Quilt Software (EQ7). In 2013, she entered her first original design at her local county fair and won "Best in Show." That made her realize that she had a real talent in designing quilts. In 2016, she devoted most of her time to pattern design. With this decision, Tina changed her business name, and this is how Quilting Affection Designs evolved into a pattern design company.

Through the years, Tina has worked with both Timeless Treasures and Island Batik. She has had quilts featured in both Spring/Summer and Fall/Winter Island Batik Catalogs in 2016. In 2017, Tina had blocks featured in the Quiltmaker's 100 Blocks Volume 15 and 16 magazines. In the Summer of 2018, she became a Studio 180 Design Certified Instructor (CI), and now all her quilt designs are created with the Studio 180 Design tools in mind. Also, as a CI, Tina teaches the tools regularly. Starting in 2019, she became a Certified Instructor with Sue Pelland Designs as well. Having both certifications enables her to write patterns that combine the two worlds of applique and piecing.

Tina is married, has two adult children, and two little Schnoodles Anna and Lucy, who help her in her Quilting Studio every day. Currently, she and her family live in Waldorf, Maryland.

Visit the author online and follow on Social Media!

Website:
quiltingaffection.com

Facebook and Instagram:
@quiltingaffectiondesigns

Made in the USA
Coppell, TX
16 December 2020